First Published in Great Britain 1993 by
Dalesman Publishing Company Limited,
Stable Courtyard, Broughton Hall,
Skipton, North Yorkshire BD23 3AE
Text © 1993 **W. R. Mitchell**

Cover picture: Upper Swaledale, photographed by **Simon Warner**

ISBN 1 85568 064 5
Typeset by **Lands Services**
Printed by **Biddles Limited**

Contents

An Introduction

Forty-five years ago, I sauntered into the Royal Oak Hotel at Settle, in the West Riding of Yorkshire, intent on interviewing Owd Mick, one of the last of the Dales drovers – a man known locally as a "bull walloper". It was to be my first article on joining Harry J. Scott at *The Dalesman*.

Mick's main claim to fame was his reputed ability to drink twelve pints of ale to twelve strokes of the clock. An old injury to his throat meant that he no longer had to waste valuable drinking time in gulping. I don't think that anyone saw him live up to his reputation – but he was kept well supplied with ale by curious visitors.

I subsidised Mick to the extent of five pints. My *Dalesman* feature was illustrated by a Horner photograph showing Mick, looking positively angelic, sitting on the doorstep of his cottage in Chapel Street.

Since that article was published, Mick has "gone to his rest" (buried in that part of Giggleswick churchyard "where there's a tree and I can hear the birds sing") and I have contributed to *The Dalesman* over a million words about Yorkshire and its people.

This county is vast and varied. At its heart is York Minster, built of Tadcaster limestone, complimenting the chalk of the Wolds – a crescent of chalk extending from south of the Humber to a dramatic termination in the white cliffs of Bempton and Flamborough.

Further north, the sea cliffs are grand but darker in hue, the north-east hinterland being dominated by the North York Moors – a hundred thousand acres of heather and bogland, grooved by small valleys which the Norsefolk called dales. Westwards are the Pennines, Defoe's "wall of brass".

Yorkshire folk are as varied as the terrain. They are bound to each other by county pride. Yorkshire fishermen sail the short, sharp sea off the north-east coast in cobles, which at other times lie on an open beach. The coble has been described as "boat and harbour in one".

Yorkshire miners inhabit pit villages, some of which are ringed by corn-fields. Yorkshire milltowners inhabit stone forests and the cricketers in white flannels stand out against the dark shades of old factories. The Dales farmer, with crook in hand and dog at foot, bestrides a broad Pennine fellside while attending to his sheep.

This anthology can give little more than a flavour of what I have seen and heard while wandering between Whitby and Waddington, Sedbergh and Spurn Point.

The Dalesman is now 54 years old and, I trust, as lively as ever . . .

PEOPLE TALKING

Alf Wight, alias James Herriot

Alf Wight (his surname spelt as in the Isle of Wight) was born in Sunderland but reared in Glasgow. "I'm a city lad," he remarked as we settled down in his study.

Bodie, a Border terrier, lay quietly under his chair. The dog was said to be eight and a-half years old, but looked older. "The Border terriers go white very early. They always look older than they really are . . ."

He had just retired from his veterinary work. Crushed by the publicity arising from the books, he had not written another story for years. Now he had a word processor. "I write when I feel like it. I do a little bit at a time. I am finding, once again, that writing's fun . . ."

A Dales Farmer Muck-spreading (Constance Pearson)

When James Herriot began work as a Dales vet, he marvelled at the stoicism of the Dalesfolk. It has been my pleasure over many years to visit the daleheads, where life is still a struggle against an unfriendly landscape and the long, long winter.

His love affair with the Yorkshire Dales began in 1940 when, having been qualified as a veterinary surgeon for less than a year, he found himself in a world which seemed for the moment to be adequately supplied with vets. He had hoped to join a busy town practice. Instead, he leapt at a chance to work at Thirsk.

"I think there was a chap called Hardwick who told somebody who told me about the job. So I dashed off to Thirsk and I got it – thank heavens!" He began work for four pounds a week.

I had not seen the vet-turned-scribbler since the launch of his book, *James Herriot's Yorkshire*, just ten years before. Also at the launch in Leeds was his wife Joan (who became Helen in the Dales stories) and their family, Jimmy and Rosemary.

The James Herriot with whom I now came face-to-face looked contented and relaxed. His face was "a good colour", as we say in Yorkshire, partly because he had been out and about, in the garden or on the hills, during most of a long sunny spell.

When I mentioned "colour", he laughed and recalled his young days as a vet visiting the dalehead farms with their memorable residents. "When they said you'd a bad colour, you got worried. I'm not a very ruddy individual really, but they would say: 'Thou's lost a bit o' ground since I saw you last, Mr. Wight.' Or: 'I think you've failed a bit, you know'."

Thirsk was "a very quiet little place". The practice he joined was presided over by the man who James Herriot was to immortalise as Siegfried Farnon. "We had a partner called Frank Bingham, a famous vet in Leyburn. (I call him Ewan Ross in my books). The trouble with Frank was that it was just at the beginning of the tuberculin-testing scheme. He couldn't do it, being 58 years old, whereas I was just 24. So they called on us at Thirsk to provide another man. That was the start of my contact with the Dales."

Frank Bingham was a tall, handsome Irishman. "Like a lot of the vets in those days, he liked a drink. Many apocryphal tales are told about him. But he was a wonderful chap, one of my favourite men. He was very kind to me."

Originally, the young vet visited Leyburn three days a week, setting off from Thirsk at about 6 a.m. and returning the same evening after a busy day in the Dales. Frank, his Swiss wife and two sons lived at a small house called *Tyrella*. Mrs Bingham is recalled as a most talented lady. She served up some wonderful meals.

James Herriot travelled about the Dales in "a funny old Austin 10". All vets were impecunious in every way. "This car had no heater, of course. The floor was broken and every time I went over a puddle the muddy water would splash up into my face. The windscreen had become so cracked that there was only one or two places I could peer through.

"Amazingly, it took me on my rounds up hill and down dale. There was one terrible period when the brakes did not work. We couldn't get around to sorting out them, so I drove all over those hilly places without being able to use them.

"I put a bit in my book about travelling into West Witton from the moortop and negotiating that terrible hairpin bend without any brakes on the car. I wouldn't do that if you gave me a million pounds now." He pondered for a moment or two and added: "I was young and tireless."

In the early 1940s, the vet had little to help him and he came across farmers who were using some methods not far removed from Black Magic. "That was probably what motivated me to write a book in the first place. It was a very funny time in veterinary practice."

James Herriot mentioned "all those awful old treatments." A cow went down. The farmer would say it had "a worm in its tail". The cow couldn't get up so he cut its tail off. "Another farmer kept a billy goat (which stank) in the shippon to prevent contagious abortion. He thought the smell would help cure the complaint. Yet abortion hit a herd only once. Then the animal developed an immunity. The herd was alright next year. The billy goat got the credit."

It was while motoring over Bellerby Moor, from Leyburn to Grinton, that James Herriot was first struck by the beauty of the Dales. He had stopped his car to let out the dog. He sat down and looked back, along the valley of the Swale towards Richmond. "I felt as though I had suddenly been transported into a magical land..."

Dales farms were so isolated the people loved to see somebody from the outside world. "They were generally large families. After I had done the 'test', they would say 'Come in and have a bit o' dinner'. This was the great saying...They were so hospitable. Everyone would 'down tools' and sit round and look at me. This was before the agricultural reps were going round."

A Dales kitchen was "a big flagged place. Enormous. You couldn't help but feel sorry for the women who had to work in such a cold draughty place. The farmer's wife who opened the door very often had an apron made of sacking. Sometimes she had clogs on her feet."

Entering the kitchen, Young Mr. Herriot would see "one of those low, brown earthenware sinks. To use it was almost literally back-breaking. There'd be a black range with an old reckon they pulled out and hung the kettle on. They made some wonderful Yorkshire puddings. I remember that."

Huge sides of fat bacon hung from hooks driven into the ceiling. "You had to duck your head to avoid brushing against them. Bacon was what they lived on. Every time you went into a kitchen, there was this lovely smell of bacon being cooked. But the fact of it was, it was nearly all fat. And I can't eat fat."

The hardiness of the dalesmen amazed him. "I was in my twenties. I'd see a fellow in his 70s shovelling away in the teeth of a cutting wind. 'It's blowing a bit thin this morning,' he would say. He'd just have a jacket on

and I'd a muffler and a heavy overcoat.
"The Dalesfolk in those days were hardy folk . . ."

(1990)

Bill Foggitt, Amateur Weatherman

He was pleased to see an emissary of *The Dalesman*. We published his first article, since when – thanks largely to television – he had become famous as a man who forecast the weather according to natural happenings in the countryside.

We chatted at the Foggitt family home, South Villa, Thirsk. Bill Foggitt has the proverbial "fund of stories". Asked by a Yorkshire editor to submit an article containing memories of life in Yorkshire, he was delighted to oblige. The editor added: "People would like to know a bit about your past." Bill replied: "Well, keep it away from the Methodists."

He was referring to his drinking habits. In this respect he obeys the Nonconformist dictum of "moderation in all things". He has a daily pilgrimage to his favourite "local" where, with a few friends, he quaffs some ale.

He had drunk "a couple o' pints" on the morning of my visit and on his return home had a "lie down". I had disturbed Bill's sleep. A neighbour ushered me into the living room and returned shortly afterwards with a cup of tea.

Bill's day begins at his home when he clambers out of bed at 7 a.m., having been roused by his dog Polly, who sleeps on his bed. Polly usually waits until the mail has arrived before taking action.

Bill records the weather – maximum and minimum temperature, rainfall and a brief comment on the day, such as "sunny, no wind". The details are taken daily and submitted to the Met. Office monthly. Not long before my visit, he had received a special award in acknowledgement of his family's 75 years of weather recording.

He doesn't have much breakfast, confining himself to cereal and coffee. "I have my own shopping to do; I live a mile out and walk across the field. And, of course, I have some refreshment at The Three Tuns at 11 o'clock. Then I come back." Betty Cook, his neighbour for 25 years, makes him a two-course meal in the evening.

Bill has been a Methodist local preacher for 52 years. His half century of service was formally recognised. "I was quite honoured; the chapel was packed . . . The president of the Conference had been the week before and he'd had a congregation of only 34. I got over a hundred!"

He was not boasting. This is Bill's own special blend of quiet humour. Many of the tales he tells are against himself. One of his best friends, a Methodist minister, takes him for runs in the car. "Last week, he took me to my old school, Scarborough College. Course, I never did anything at school. I could write and I was good at natural history, but you didn't get a job through that."

Scarborough College is now a "mixed school". As he said ruefully, recalling the all-boy days, he was "born out of due time, like St. Paul." The two visitors from Thirsk were shown round the school by a stylish young lady who said: "Walk this way, please." Bill had promptly replied: "We'll try."

He is 78 years old and comes from a long-lived family. His father told him: "You could live to a good age and, even if you don't, you won't die from overwork and rushing around." When invited to take part in a radio programme, he was ushered into the presence of Derek Jameson, a Media celebrity, Bill was asked what he did when he worked. "I never worked," he replied. "Eh," said the Cockney interviewer. "I wish I'd known you all those years ago; we could have gone into partnership."

At a time when everyone was talking about the Greenhouse Effect, and an over-heating of the earth, Bill commented: "It'll be a long time before it's a matter of Thirsk-by-the-Sea. The waves'll have to get over Sutton Bank." He had been telling television audiences we are more likely to be advancing towards a Little Ice Age.

Bill is lean and lish [nimble]. He grew up at a time when young people were not allowed to be bored. His mother told him to keep his mind "occupied". His father was a chemist. "He would never see a doctor – not even when he was dying." Father was pretty fit all his life, though he had no hair. "That was a let-down, being a chemist."

When Bill was a lad, on market day he saw the stalls of cheapjacks right in front of his father's shop. One man described himself as a "hair-restorer". He was quick to point out Dad's baldness, which was a poor recommendation for the type of "restorer" he sold.

Bill receives a little help with the housework, but not on a Monday. He looked at me, his face creasing with the onset of a laugh and he remarked: "So, whatever else happens, I mustn't die on a Monday."

(1991)

John Hillaby: Walker and Author

When the jets of low-flying military aircraft were sucking the feathers from grouse and curlews on other parts of the North York Moors, it was quiet – very quiet – around Rosedale, where John Hillaby has a cottage. He said: "I love deserts . . . I thank God that there is a sufficient degree of detachment here to enable us to hear a sheepdog break wind in Farndale."

We talked our way back down the years to what he called The Great

Melt, "when tongues of ice came across from Scandinavia and gave up in despair when they crashed against the cliffs of Cliff-land [Cleveland], the Viking name for the north-western edge of the moors."

Those moors must originally have been clothed in really good stands of Scots pine. To this well-timbered area came the Maglemosians (the Big Bog People), who left southern Scandinavia, particularly Denmark. "They paddled and poled their way across what is now the North Sea and was then a gigantic swamp" and found on these moors more hospitable conditions than they left behind.

John Hillaby switched the subject to the ubiquitous sheep, the moor-jocks. That morning, at about seven o'clock, he had looked out of his cottage window only to see twenty or thirty "jocks" cheerfully champing his precious collection of heathers – a collection he had built up over a number of years.

"I think that many people in Rosedale resent the fact that some of our

Solitary Walker near Blakey Topping (Alec Wright)

From his home in Rosedale, John Hillaby has frequently set out alone to follow the old moorland tracks. I, too, have been alone but never lonely in the wild places of Yorkshire, where one might sense the ghosts of packmen, monks and miners.

flockmasters, by not keeping their gates and walls in good order, are free-booters – a polite word for "fodder-thieves". I appreciated his problem, and was much too polite to ask him if he had considered fencing the garden against the sheep.

The moorgate is about fifty yards from John Hillaby's cottage. His garden is some sixteen paces in length, from the front door of his home to the gate. Like the moor, the garden has an acid soil; it sustains umpteen varieties of heather. Among them are a Yorkshire threesome – cross-leaved heather, bell heather and ling.

In clear, sunny conditions, I contemplated Rosedale, which John Hillaby referred to as "a deeply-dissected dale which would be called a combe in Devon and a cwm in Wales." Far below me was the principal settlement, Rosedale Abbey, usually called T'Abbey.

Rosedale has tended to be a dale of freeholders, with much changing of ownership of the various properties. In a Victorian industrial boom period, "Rosedale was the Klondyke of north-eastern England." On to an old farming community, in a few hectic years, was grafted a mining people, and the population soared to 3,000 (it is currently not quite 200).

Said John: "The iron was exploited sideways. Labour was cheap, and to Rosedale came mine workers from Aberdeen to Cornwall. They all converged in those dreadful days when a man just thanked God to get the price of bread to keep his children alive."

It was a halcyon time for the local fleas. With shift working in operation, an incoming worker immediately settled in a bed which had been vacated by a friend. Many a bed was never allowed to become cold.

John said that miners walked to the mines from Lastingham, Hutton-le-Hole, Danby, Glaisdale and Commondale, "converging like bees at a hive on those two great iron workings in Rosedale. They had to be underground at six o' clock in the morning or else they were 'stood down'."

The device which summoned them to work was t'whistle or buzzer. "Arthur Champion, who now lives at Castleton, got the buzzer going for me," John recalled. "He dragged it out, set it up and used compressed air rather than steam to make it work. Arthur gave me twenty minutes and I walked back towards home. Then I could hear this strange moaning noise. In the old days, a man knew that if he was not in the mine when the buzzer sounded, he was out of a day's work."

I motored back up the side of Rosedale, by way of the notorious Bank, and crossed the moor to Hutton-le-Hole. The moor-jocks were continuing their age-old task of keeping the moorland vegetation low.

I hoped that the burst of spring sunshine would persuade them to stay on the moors, away from John Hillaby's heathers – his bid to bring the moorland flavour to his front door.

(1982)

Donald Lee: A Man and his Bike

He was still cycling in his 80th year and he hoped that when his birthday came round he would have the energy to add 80 miles to the 300,000 he had already covered on two wheels since, as a lad, he acquired a bike advertised in *The Keighley News* for £1.

Donald Lee began cycling properly when a week's millwork brought him just over £1, and he observed: "If I'd £5 when I set off on a tour, I thowt I wor a millionaire." Donald, having returned home following a fortnight's tour of the Scottish islands, counted up the remaining "brass" and found he had spent the grand total of £4.6s.11d.

Donald was one of the last half-timers in the West Riding. In 1918, he spent half the day at school and half at work. "I was at t'mill afore six o'clock on my twelfth birthday," he says in a speech which is richly endowed with the dialect of his native valley.

Cycling offered a working man and woman a relatively cheap way of escaping from the grimy home acres into the Dales or up to the Lakes. "We'd go up t'Dales in an hour or two. We used to take sandwiches for dinner-time and called at one of t'Cyclists' Touring Club places for a pot of tea – which cost fourpence." If somebody found a "thruppenny shop", he'd go ten miles of out his way to save a penny.

The cyclists of the 1920s toured on "ten bob a day". Those travelling up the Dales pedalled briskly to a point north of Skipton "where they started on limestone roads which were either dusty or puddly. If they went over Fleet Moss, or on any of those high roads, they had lots o'gates to oppen. I seem to remember eight or nine gates across t'track from Stainforth to Halton Gill. They were rough roads. It was just as well to learn how to mend a puncture before you set off."

The CTC *Handbook* was a touring cyclist's bible. "In the early 1930s, a cyclist who wanted bed and breakfast was in competition with a motorist. He belonged to t'AA, but carried our *Handbook*. If you saw him, you'd got to beat him to it!"

In the early days, a cyclist had a choice between an oil lamp and an acetylene lamp to provide light for the homeward ride. Some small paraffin lamps were called Bobby Dodgers. "Acetylene lamps were t'best; they gave a longer beam. I was once going down Fleet Moss at midnight when a rabbit started running at side o' t'bike. All of a sudden, it darted across, got knocked down and killed. I took it home, of course. It were etten. We never left nowt like that on t'road."

The lady at one guest house told the cyclists, at breakfast-time that she had been up until one o'clock drying the cyclists' sodden clothes and equipment. "She must have had my cycling shoes in t'oven, because later on they brok across middle. Those shoes were hard-baked."

On stormy days, the cyclists from Keighley might go no further than the Mallinsons, of the Fox and Hounds at Starbotton, in Upper Wharfedale, here to laik [play] pontoon for safety matches. "We took a pack of cards with us. You owt to hev heard t'arguments that were going. Talk about rogues and twisters! I said to one chap who later started his own textile business: 'Looking back, I bet thou argued more over t'matches than thou does ower tharsands o' pounds worth o'yarn today.' He said: 'It's a fact.'"

Donald wonders how the caterer made any profit at all. Mr Wade, a baker, had a house at Halton East where the cyclists sometimes went to play cards all Sunday afternoon. "Pontoon for matches, it was. They always kept a good fire, and had all t'leets burnin'. They earned eightpence at the most, on some days . . ."

Donald leaned back, reflected and then added: "Four old pence! That's all they got . . ."

(1986)

Dick Cresswell: the Swaledale Bobby

He could not believe his good fortune when he was given the task of policing 88,000 acres of moor and dale which comprise the largest beat for a single officer in England. Dick Cresswell, a native of Ingleton, was patrolling a large part of what has become known to tourists as the Herriot Country.

A recent early morning telephone call from a Dales farmer informed Dick that a small group of poachers was operating in the dale. Theoretically, the Swaledale Bobby was off duty, but he decided the easiest course was to investigate the report himself or there might be another telephone call to report a more serious offence, such as burglary.

Dick is more than familiar with the poaching fraternity – with men from the North East towns who, driving "old bangers" and having nets or lamps and lurchers, turn off the Great North Road to Scotch Corner and pass through Richmond to go rabbitting in the Dales. About 98 per cent of the men have criminal records. "You don't get their sort of criminal record just for poaching."

In Swaledale, they have no choice of roads. "It's a matter of one way in, one way out," observes Dick. The poachers are not especially clever. If they slip through Dick's hands he can soon contact his colleagues at Richmond. They will keep an eye open for the poachers' cars as they are driven homewards.

The ideal night for poaching is dark and windy. "The poachers are not very proficient. I know there are a lot of rabbits about, but they don't catch very many. They don't care what they do and where they go; they put a light on, locate a rabbit and run the animal down with a lurcher, which is a 'sight' hound crossed with a herding dog. The usual cross is three-parts greyhound and one-part collie."

One Sunday morning, Dick was called to Marrick, where two local farmers had blocked in a car suspected of being used by poachers. "There was a tractor at one side and a Land Rover at the other. I looked into the car and saw a ferret box on the back seat.

"A chap came walking up. He had nothing with him. 'Is this your car, sir?' 'Yes.' 'Have you bin doing a spot of poaching?' 'No.' 'What are you doing with a ferret box in the back of your car?' He replied: 'Well, you can't catch rabbits with a ferret box."

One of the farm lads had a hunch where the man had been. I said: 'Have you anyone else with you?' He said: 'No.' A suspicious-looking man was standing on the road, looking over the wall. A motor bike trial was going on in another field. He gave the impression he was looking at that.

"I drove towards him, wound down the window of my car and said: 'Your mate wants you back at his car.' 'Oh, all right,' he says. So I took him back and said: 'Come on, lads, you'd best be out of the parish.'"

Dick's career began at Richmond, continued at Bedale and is now in full bloom in Swaledale, where the job satisfaction is considerable in the company of genuine folk and a backdrop of glorious hills, each of which Dick has climbed either for pleasure or while assisting the voluntary Swaledale Fell Rescue Association.

He does not care much for cities, though his wife Pat reminded him that he had been to London – once! Dick queried this and added: "I've been down there twice – you don't need to tell me about London!"

In common with his colleagues in other parts of the Dales, he receives calls about "missing" walkers and usually asks the inquirer what time the "missing" man – it's invariably a man – is due back and what route he is likely to take. Quite often the reply to the latter question is: "Oh, via Muker and on to Keld."

At this stage, Dick asks: "Have you tried the pub?" "No." "Well just hang on a minute." Dick promptly rings up the local pub and speaks to the landlord, asking him to announce the name of the missing person. Invariably, when the landlord returns to the telephone, he says: "Your 'missing' man has just picked up his rucksack and he's on his way back."

In the winter of 1984-85, a four-wheel drive car proved its worth on the snowbound moorland roads when motorists came slitheringly to a halt and must be rescued. One day, Dick brought nine people to safety. "All nine piled into my Subaru car. I returned with the snow plough less than fifteen minutes later to try and free the cars, only to find the drifts were too much for it."

That same winter, a retired clergyman living at Redmire was taking services at Muker. On a funeral day, snow was falling as he set off to cross the moors. He did not turn up at the appointed time and Dick Cresswell set off to investigate. He found the clergyman's car had slithered off the road and was now resting with its front end in a ditch.

"I followed footprints in the snow and caught up with him about a mile from his car. His long coat was flapping in the wind as he made his way home. He was not a very happy man because, as he explained, in all his years as a clergyman he had yet to miss attending a service.

Dick assisted him to keep an unblemished record by driving him to his funeral service. "I returned with a friend of mine to the stranded car, put a rope on it, hitched up the car and drew it on to the road. We managed to have that car available at the end of the service."

The clergyman took the low road home.

(1990)

YORKSHIRE SKYLINES

Roseberry Topping:
the Matterhorn of Cleveland

Margery Moorpoot, a character in an 18th century play about the Cleveland area of north-east Yorkshire, described Roseberry Topping as "t'biggest hill i' all Yorkshur." She was reflecting a notion held by people who did not travel far from home, living their quiet lives in the shadow of this miniature Matterhorn. Surely, no Yorkshire hill could be taller.

The visual impact of Roseberry Topping is much greater than its elevation of 1,057 ft would suggest. From a distance, it resembles a giant molar on a gum of green. At close range, as from the road between Great Ayton and Newton, it appears to block out half the sky.

Margery Moorpoot claimed that "it's aboon a mahle an a hawf heegh, an' as cawd as ice at t'top on 't, i' t'yattest day i' summer, that it is." The exaggeration is understandable.

Distant View of Roseberry Topping (Alec Wright)

It dominates the skyline with a conspicuousness which is out of all proportion to its size. It is no wonder that local people used to claim it as the highest hill in all Yorkshire. A hilltop view of the Plain always reminds me of the couplet: "Cleveland in the Clay, /Take two boots, bring one away."

Roseberry Topping, soaring from the edge of the Plain, appears to dominate the area and the much plainer Easby Moor, which is fractionally higher and has the additional height of an obelisk raised in memory of Captain James Cook, the circumnavigator.

Little Roseberry is, in comparison with its two neighbours, a green pimple on the escarpment.

I travelled to Roseberry Topping in an April drought. Sheep and their new lambs were panting in the heat and the big arable fields were as lushly green as municipal lawns. Walkers on Roseberry Topping raised puffs of dust at every footfall.

The hillside oakwoods held the sheen of new leaves and the alluring hue of massed bluebells. The open hillside above was spangled with the gold of flowering gorse. In clear conditions, I could have seen the sea to the east and the bastions of Wensleydale to the far west. It was hazy, but the seaside flavour was provided by fulmar petrels sailplaning beside the crags or croaking while resting on their tarsii.

My companions on the climb were Bob and Jenny Dicker. He had just been appointed warden-in-charge for the North York Moors properties of the National Trust but was already familiar with Roseberry Topping, recalling an ascent in snowtime, when the hill gleamed. For Jenny, the most memorable climb was partly on all-fours as a strong wind battered the shelterless slopes.

"Roseberry" appears to be derived from a Norse name, meaning Odin's mountain. Old writers mentioned "Newton under Oseberry". To Camden, a 17th century geographer, "it is a landmark that directs sailors, and a prognostic of weather to the neighbours", who were doubtless guided by the couplet:

> When Roseberrye Toppinge wears a cappe
> Let Cleveland then beware a clappe.

The county boundary (North Yorkshire/Cleveland) splits the face of the Topping and the National Trust own 250 acres on the Cleveland side. Our ascent included a detour to visit The Shooting Box, a stone structure maybe 200 years old which the North Yorkshire Moors National Park authority had restored.

The Topping, which looked so substantial from a distance, had at closer range a careworn appearance, brought about by ironstone mining. Just over a century ago, the Pease family of Darlington rented from the Staveley family "the mines and seams of ironstone and iron ore under all lands in the parish of Newton with power to search, sink shafts, erect buildings and carry away the ore."

Until 1914, Roseberry Topping was conical. Then the southern half of the peak collapsed in a mass of sandstone blocks, creating a more interesting shape.

Eventually, we reached the flat summit. The top six feet of the hill lie outside the tract owned by the National Trust. I sat and watched the fulmars making use of a light breeze as they glided backwards and forwards, scarcely moving their wings.

Camden, ascending the hill in clear weather, wrote of "a most goodly prospecte from the toppe of this hyll, though paynefully gayned by reason of the steepness of yt." He viewed "the vale and pastures and the sea replenished with shippes."

The Topping, "t'biggest hill i' all Yorkshur", is a natural grandstand.

(1987)

Three Peaks in a Day

Our 25-mile circuit, taking in the summit cairns of Penyghent, Whernside and Ingleborough, and involving 5,000 ft of climbing, began with a queue for a stile at Brackenbottom and ended with a jog-trot down Sulber Nick.

The walk had a charitable objective – to provide a trained dog for a blind person – otherwise I would not have ventured on to such an over-used path, where rocks have been scuffed by boots and stretches of soft ground transformed by boot-power into a porridge-like mush of peat and clay.

When I first walked the Three Peaks, with Ken Pounder, it was not easy to find the best route on an unlacerated landscape. We could not ask anyone the way because we were the only people doing it that day. Now my companions were two compulsive walkers – Charlie Emett from Darlington and his pal Bill from Durham.

We met at the Penyghent Cafe in Horton to "clock in". My card showed 8-10 a.m. The stile at Brackenbottom proved to be a bottleneck, but soon the youngest and daftest Three Peakers were in rapid ascent of the foothills of Penyghent. A skylark sang, a meadow pipit descended in "shuttlecock" display flight and from the mossland came the chittering of a snipe.

As we climbed, our view of Penyghent changed. The hill lost its lion-like shape. Soon, having negotiated a ladder stile, we beheld the lower part of the slope leading to the head of Penyghent. "That's not all, lad," said a doleful West Yorkshireman, to one of his winded companions. The doleful one added: "Tha can't even see top 'alf from 'ere!"

Young people from Boston Spa, and a dog which was gripping a large stone with its teeth, overtook me on the steepest bit. A raven drifted by. The terrestrial reception committee was formed of a Dales-bred ewe and its two hefty lambs. The ewe nuzzled my rucksack, demanding food.

Three Peakers long since broke away from the recognised right of way between Penyghent and Ribblehead. The sign to Horton was ignored. Successive parties went directly ahead, ultimately through a Flanders-like

Ingleborough from Chapel-de-Dale (Maurice Barringer)

*John Ruskin, looking at the best-known of the Three Peaks as he journeyed
up the valley from Ingleton on a breezy day, marvelled how Ingleborough could
stand without rocking. Forty years ago, having climbed to see the new
windbreak, I found an aspidistra in a pot, with a note which, it was claimed, had
been written by Gracie Fields.*

terrain, by way of Black Dub, Moss bog and Red Moss bog to the Promised
Landscape of the dalehead.

A middle-aged man fell into Hull Pot Beck. A young walker sank to his
waist in cloying peat during what turned out to be a classic case of bog-
hopping. I was overtaken by three young men who had but one rucksack.
Each wore it for half an hour and then passed it to the next on the rota.

There was respite on the firmer ground via God's Bridge and a dusty
white track from Nether Lodge to Lodge Hall. Braving main road traffic,
we strode to Ribblehead, here to take the pressure off the boots and to
be comforted by circulation returning to our feet and legs. A grey-haired
motorist who gathered that it was not the first time we had been on
the Three Peaks circuit said, brightly: "Oh – you know what you're in
for then!"

Then we were off to Whernside on a route which, beyond the crossing
of the railway, was a climb through another peatscape, tramping over
experimental strips of durable material laid by the Three Peaks Project,
a scheme aimed at making the main footpaths more durable.

Whernside, the least popular of the Three Peaks, was depressing that
day. The Weather Clerk had mustered grey cloud and a wind. The
whistling of golden plover seemed sadder than ever. The summit of
Whernside, re-seeded with grass, had since been scoured by boots.

The recommended way off the fell, towards Chapel-le-Dale, held the remnants of a system of steps which had become a major hazard for the unwary or those with wobbly legs.

A most pleasant surprise was the state of the path through the Nature Conservancy ground on the western side of our third peak, Ingleborough. Beyond Southerscales reserve, and stretching to the bottom of the near-vertical stretch on the ridge, lay a flexible board walk. I overheard a walker say: "They might have gone the whole hog and put in an escalator."

The state of the final climb had been improved by positioning large stones to form irregular steps. On the misty summit plateau of Ingleborough, I placed a stone on the highest part of the cairn. We three walkers then celebrated our attaining the top of Ingleborough with a special meal – orangeade and dried prunes!

The path down to Horton had been given a durable surface. It passed the remains of the shooting hut and followed Sulber Nick, in the grand setting of limestone pavements. I clocked in at the Penyghent Cafe with perhaps ten minutes to spare.

A pint of hot coffee and a buttered scone brought the colour back into my face.

(1992)

Ilkley Moor: A Splendid Wilderness

The lad who courted Mary Jane on Ilkley Moor is nameness, but most of the world knows about him through the somewhat grisly song which became a Yorkshire anthem. He went to Ilkla' Moor baht 'at [without a hat] and ran the risk of catching his deeath o' cowd and being buried, to become food, in turn, for worms, ducks and humans.

What started out as an example of bawdy West Riding humour can be sung lustily and easily at communal efforts, largely because of the catchy tune, originally a hymn tune called *Cranbrook*.

I wore a hat on Ilkley Moor (Yorkshiremen do not make the same daft mistake twice) but a gale-force wind lifted the hat, carrying it for a few hundred yards until it lodged against millstone grit, an outcropping lump of coarse brown rock which rose above the litter of last year's bracken crop.

The wind that day was the grandfather of all Pennine blasts. On the journey up from town to the Cow and Calf Rocks it not only rocked the car but produced a tuba-like solo by forcing itself through a fine crack between a side window and its frame.

Later I leaned against the blast, baht 'at, but have lived to tell the tale of Ilkley Moor – a 1,700 acre slab of rough, high land, sprouting heather, crowberry, bracken and bent.

A few clumps of pines cling desperately to the ridges. There are boggy places where one might easily sink up to the knees in peat and sphagnum moss. Along the edges of the Moor are signs of man's activity in the little farmsteads. A flattened area near the Cow and Calf Rocks, is intended for car-parking. Until the 1939-45 war, an 18-hole golf course was laid out near Panorama.

The demarcation between the Moor and town is sudden and (since cattle grids were fitted to the high roads) quite decisive. The moor sheep once found their richest grazings in local gardens, with a partiality for wallflowers. On a single disastrous night, sheep ate about £100 of prize carnations in a garden.

Ilkley Moor is not a precise enough term for those who have to administer it. In the byelaws, the expression "the moor" means Ilkley Moor, Holling Hall Moor, Panorama Rocks, Heber's Ghyll and "all waste and other land" described in the conveyance of 1893 from Marmaduke Francis Middleton to the Ilkley Local Board.

The Moor rises to an elevation of 1,320 ft. Pennine rain has formed watercourses in places like Spicey Gill and Willy Hall Spout. They replenish The Tarn which lies between Troutbeck Hotel and Craiglands – a tarn on which skating regularly took place during old-fashioned winters.

Cow and Calf Rocks, at the edge of Ilkla' Moor (A.P. Waterhouse)

A Victorian ballad about a lad who went hatless to this tract of moorland when courtin' Mary Jane has become the Yorkshire anthem. The millfolk of Airedale tramped across the moor during their limited time off work. Gritstone outcrops bear the cup-and-ring marks of an ancient people.

The fame of Ilkley Moor is not based solely on an old ballad, which was composed impromptu during the visit of a West Riding choir and set to the familiar hymn tune. Up there on the moor are mysterious carved stones, one carving having the shape of a swastika. Re-discovered in the 1870s, it is now protected by barbed wire and railings. There is a copy of it in the Manor House Museum in Ilkley.

Scores of carved stones, some of them bearing "cup and ring" symbols, dating back thousands of years, have been recorded on the Yorkshire moors. Mid-Wharfedale is a particularly good place in which to see them.

It is an eerie sensation to come across such markings, made by the first human occupants of the area, in this Yorkshire wilderness, with its bold outcrops of millstone grit, its rustling bracken, ling and bogland.

(1967)

Greenhow Hill: Half Way to Heaven

When, towards the the end of last century, the Rev. J. M. Chadwick was appointed vicar of Greenhow, between Pateley Bridge and Grassington, a dalesman conveying him by horse and trap up the Banks from Pateley told the new parson: "Well! It's as near heaven as ever you'll get . . . Aye! T'view's varry fine, but tha cannot ait [eat] it!"

At Stone's Hill, the gradient is 1 in 6 (some say, 1 in 5) and the incline at Strawberry Hill and the formidable Red Brae tilt the car of a modern visitor so that the driver has a view mainly of the big sky.

The road crests at 1,326 ft. The lych gate of Greenhow's burial ground is inscribed with familiar words, "I will lift up mine eyes to the hills", though you actually look down on them. What goes up must come down, and in due course the road makes a spectacular dip on its way to Hebden and Grassington.

One of Kipling's "soldiers three" was to remember the heights of Greenhow for the tewits [lapwings], which manage to hang on to their plumage in the stiff breezes. Harald Bruff, who wrote about the doings of Greenhow folk, mentioned that the wind "blows fresh and is laden with the fragrance of ling bloom, bent grass and wet moss, the true moor mixture."

When there's mist and drizzle on Greenhow, the housewives of Pateley may be hanging out washing in clear conditions. When those same house-wives are in autumn mist, the sun may be lighting up the hilltop.

The road over Greenhow has a wild setting. Northwards, a tract of moor-land, pockmarked by old lead mine workings, extends for some ten miles to Great Whernside. It is said that a clear-weather view from High Crag, near Stump Cross takes in the towers of York Minster, over thirty miles away.

The road over Greenhow is an ancient route. This way came the Romans, interested in local veins of lead. It was a route followed by monks. In due course, it became part of a turnpike originating in Knaresborough.

At Greenhow, the houses are like stones on a necklace, with the main road as the thread. The settlement took shape in the seventeenth century, when miners who had been trudging up the Banks each working day were permitted to build cottages on moorland "intakes" and live near their work.

Some miners continued to walk, and a Victorian miner recalled by my old (and now late lamented) friend, Fred Longthorn, arrived on the Hill at 5-30 a.m. and rested for half an hour before joining the shift, which began at 6 a.m.

With the great days of lead-mining over, the spoil-heaps were rifled for fluorspar, which was sold for steel-making. Wooden "slippers" were used to arrest the two-wheeled carts in their descent of the Banks. A "slipper", a wedge-shaped piece of wood attached to the body of the cart by a chain, was "slipped" under the cart wheel, causing it to slur. The squealing sound of a braked cart was excruciating.

Oade Will, Fred Longthorn's father, who died in 1933, had taken a horse and cart from Greenhow to Skipton to collect coal. He would set off from home at 5 a.m. and (fearing robbers) he usually slipped his money into his clogs.

Greenhow Hill has its ghosts, one of whom was first reported at the time of the Luddite troubles in Lancashire, when soldiers were force-marched over Greenhow from their base in Yorkshire to help to quell the disturbances.

A group of men came this way on such a hot day that one of their number, John Kay, developed sunstroke. His friends bathed his head, but John died. He was buried by the road and local people reared a stone at his head and feet to mark the spot. They were reputed to have left a musket beside the body.

In subsequent years, Greenhow folk, when passing the two stones, "danked" their clogs to make the metal ring, at the same time calling out: "Gie us a knock, John Kay." Fred Longthorn and others dug down and found the skeleton, together with some brass buttons. They sent a thigh bone to the doctor at Pateley Bridge who deduced that John Kay had been an especially tall man. The grave was re-filled with earth.

The "ghost" revealed itself to a group of local people as they returned home in the early hours of a clear moonlit night, after having been on a day excursion by rail from Pateley. Strange sounds were reported by the women, who had walked ahead. The sounds came from the grave of John Kay.

A tramp had lain down to sleep, his head resting on the hummock of the grave. The tramp was snoring!

(1981)

Sheep Show at Tan Hill

I t didn't actually rain for the 28th annual show of Swaledale sheep, held at Tan Hill, some 1,730 ft above sea level, but at one stage the mist had such liquid consistency it might almost be called drizzle. The way to distinguish Pennine fog and mist is to put out your tongue and taste 'em.

I had a choice of parking places outside the hostelry, the "highest licensed premises in England". Then a farmer arrived. Asked what time the sheep show began, he replied: "Hawf past eleven. Summat like that." He reflected further and added: "Or twelve o'clock – summat like."

The appeal of the annual springtime sheep show on Tan Hill is in its informality. I am not suggesting that it is badly organised. Quite the reverse. When plans for an event have been well and truly made, there can be a relaxed atmosphere, and the average Dales farmer doesn't like a lot of fuss.

Friends had told me of the phenomenon of a vacant moor suddenly filling up with humanity at the very last moment before sheep-judging began. When the farmers did appear, mainly with Land Rovers and trailers, their names were truly of the Dales – Alderson and Raine, Harker and Calvert, Garnett and Blades.

There were two main topics – the weather and sheep. A member of the Nidderdale brass band hired for the day said, as he prepared to play in the grey murk: "Last year, it was shirt sleeves and sun glasses. Now it feels like the tail-end o' winter." A farmer remarked that the long winter had "shakken t'sheep up."

I wandered into the hostelry, the walls of which are an impressive three feet thick. Two farmers propped up the bar. "How is't?" asked one of the other, who had just arrived. "I'se nobbut livin'," was the reply.

The first man observed, gravely: "Hevn't sin you aw winter. Thowt you'd passed along." His companion said: "Nay, I'se still wick [alive]. We've summat to celebrate . . ." "Aye," was the reply, "if thou's paying for it!" And so the good-humoured banter went on, accompanied by the clink of beer glasses.

A springtime date was planned because at this time of the year, shows are uncommon. Clifford Harker, the secretary for some fourteen years, explained: "After lambing time, the farmers like a chance to have a crack about the past winter. Many haven't met each other since the October tup sales."

The dull thump of a generator could be heard from behind the inn. Tan Hill is not linked to the national electricity grid and the water supply comes from a private pump. Motorists who have journeyed for four or five miles through the lean lands of the Pennines cannot resist stopping here.

Walkers on the Pennine Way regard it as a major "watering hole".

Mine host said: "We tend to make our own weather. We're well and truly on the watershed – influenced by both east and west. We find that as we approach the inn, from either direction, the weather tends to change in the last two miles. If we've had sunshine, then the weather deteriorates. If we've had poor conditions, it'll be sunny on the Hill." That day the wind was "fresh". In the latest winter there had been twelve foot drifts of snow.

A trickle of farmers and sheep soon became a torrent. I asked a dalesman about the condition of the sheep after such a grim winter. "Nay – thou won't be able to tell at this show," he asserted. "This lot will have been in t'parlour. It's sheep out theear" – he pointed across the misty moor – "that's yardstick."

The owners made their sheep look pretty, running a damp cloth over their faces and fluffing out fleeces which had been crushed during the journey; this they did with short, quick, upward movements of the fingers. One tup had its knees washed in soapy water.

Head, carcass, coat – these were three features of a sheep that interested the judges. One of them told me: "A coat should have depth – and be a little curly on top. If you get it too fine, and there's some bad weather in winter, the coat might shed and the sheep'll be starved."

I stood with sharp-eyed farmers as the Swaledale sheep were being judged. The oldest animals had their age indicated by grey hairs about their eyes – hair which stood out against the dark faces almost as though the sheep had been provided with goggles.

There was a testiness between tups that did not know each other. Two animals faced each other, reversed for several yards, and charged, their heads meeting with a loud thwack. One tup, having been bought for £7,000, must have caused the farmer worry every time it coughed. A sheep doesn't ail for long. "It either gits better soon – or it dies."

Now the strains of Middlesmoor and Lofthouse Band could be heard and a ringing sound from the yard behind the inn indicated that the "Grand Quoits Match" was in progress. Two quoits, bands of steel, had collided on a square of puddled clay brought in from the moor "to make t'quoits stick".

In the chilly air of 1,730 ft, no queue had developed for quoits. Inside the Tan Hill Inn there were just two main topics of conversation – the weather and the sheep.

(1979)

FAVOURITE PLACES

The Strid: Where the Wharfe Goes White with Fury

I parked my car a few paces from the river, within easy viewing range of a dipper which flexed its leg muscles, doing the avian equivalent of press-ups, before taking a walk on the river bed, looking for food. The Wharfe retains its old weedy state. It has not been scoured clean by pollutants. Dipper, sandpiper, kingfisher and goosander are some of the birds that give it life.

A walk from the Cavendish Pavilion to the High Strid does not over-tax the leg muscles and it exercises the mind. This section of Wharfedale is steep-sided, rocky, half in shadow, abounding in trees, plants and birds. The highpoint of excitement comes at the famous Strid, where a powerful river is channelled by outcropping gritstone. The water, now up to thirty feet deep, seethes and frets.

The Rev William Carr, inducted as Rector of Bolton Abbey in 1789, persuaded the 6th Duke of Devonshire to open out the woods to visitors. This was the Romantic Age, a time of revolt against classicism and when those with taste and leisure were exploring (and being horror-struck by) the wilder parts of Britain.

Carr not only laid out nearly thirty miles of paths between Bolton and Barden; he provided "viewpoints", with named seats. His writings publicised the area. William Wordsworth, visiting Wharfedale in the summer of 1807, wrote that William Carr "has worked with an invisible hand of art – in the very spirit of nature."

About 40,000 people a year trudge through the woods to the Strid, using a map on which nature trails are represented by coloured lines – red, green, yellow and purple. I chose the last-named route, which brought me to the river's edge and a view of the wooded Lud Islands, an assortment of islands, the largest tailor-made for adventure and the smallest just an accumulation of muck around the roots of a tree which, like the early tourists, appears to be holding up its branches in horror.

I passed a sulphur well, with its flat "rotten egg" smell and then I was on the green trail, the main path – the M1 of Bolton Woods – which once was wide and firm enough for the passage of horse-drawn vehicles when the more affluent visitors from urban areas enjoyed a day at Bolton Abbey.

Wordsworth, beautifying a bloodthirsty little ballad, had written *The White Doe of Rylstone* and ensured that generations of visitors would continue to take a romantic view of their surroundings.

The Strid Woods cover 130 acres, on both sides of the Wharfe. John Sheard, the estate agent, mentioned the sheltered and damp condition of the Woods – a condition creating a micro-climate in which trees grow well. Little natural woodland remains and the area is managed as a much-appreciated amenity rather than on strict commercial lines.

Some fifty species of bird breed in this area. The pied flycatcher, a summer visitor, arrives towards the end of April. There may be twenty pairs nesting in the riverside trees. The goosander, one of the species of duck known as "sawbills" from serrations at the rim, is here at its most southerly breeding station in Britain.

Bolton Woods offer a balm to the mind. Artists and writers encouraged visitors to look through rose-tinted spectacles. Even the naturalists who count and classify acknowledge the special appeal of this wild little ravine in the middle of a large dale, where the river forces its way between dark beds of millstone grit.

At times, with vapour rising from the river, enveloping the trees, it has affinities with a tropical rain forest. Even little Posforth Gill, which pours its water into the Wharfe, became romanticised many years ago when a violent storm toppled many of the trees. Storms happened before and since, but that one storm took someone's fancy. The gill became known as the Valley of Desolation and so it remains, though the old wounds have long since healed.

Notes provided for school parties describe the famous Strid in O or A level terms. Here is millstone grit (the Skipton Moor Grit), a coarse sandstone containing among the quartz grains a proportion of feldspar and some pebbles. They are the earliest rocks of the Upper Carboniferous Series, E-zone and date from 325 million years.

Grit at the Strid occupies the trough of a syncline. The rocks, almost horizontal, are full of potholes, formed by the rotary action of pebbles in the rapid current of the river when in flood. Small potholes point upstream, large ones being corkscrew shaped. The deep gorge, focal point of so many romantic tales, was formed from the joining up of a succession of potholes.

I returned to the Cavendish Pavilion on the blue trail, so named after a carpet of bluebells which is visible in late string.

(1985)

Mount Grace: A Place for Stylish Living

What used to be a country lane is now the mighty A19, linking York with Teesside. What used to be country traffic has been succeeded by cars and groups of heavy lorries. As I waited to join the road, on my way to see the finest remaining example of a

Carthusian abbey, an approaching cluster of lorries and car-transporters looked as fearsome as a cavalry charge.

I had been blundering (mapless) through Yorkshire, glorying in my presence on some unfamiliar minor roads. They were leafy and winding, except where I climbed out of Nidderdale for a run across the moor by Dallowgill and Kirkby Malzeard. I returned to yet more shadowy routes between here and Masham.

This was a Yorkshire of big, sun-scorched fields littered with enormous bales of straw, leading me to the foot of the North East moorland bloc. Still blundering, I passed through Brompton, viewed Mount Grace in its wooded setting, lost sight of it round another bend of the road and passed under the A19 to reach Osmotherley.

A middle-aged sun-worshipper who had stripped as far as decency would permit, said, when I inquired about Mount Grace: "You're the third person who has lost his way this morning." The error, caused by the monstrous A19, was easily rectified.

Not being able to remove the road, I joined it and located one of those plain-chocolate tinted signposts relating to points of interest, in an area of low-flying aircraft and high-flying lorries.

That clear, oven-hot day suited the pastel shades, the reds and yellows,

Mount Grace, near Osmotherley (Alec Wright)

In the picture is a mansion, roofed with warm-toned pantiles, beyond which are the remains of a Carthusian monastery. The brothers lived like hermits but in some style and at mealtimes each had food and drink delivered by means of an L-shaped cavity, so that there should be no eye contact between those concerned.

of Mount Grace Priory. Weathered red pantiles and yellow sandstone go well together. I passed through a tower porch into the cool recesses of a Jacobean type of dwelling built by the Lascelles family in 1654 from the remains of the Priory guest house.

Beyond lay the dignified remains of the House of Assumption of the Most Blessed Virgin and St. Nicholas of Mount Grace at Ingleby – one of the nine Carthusian houses in England and undoubtedly the finest remaining example in the world.

It was founded by Thomas Duke of Surrey, a nephew of Richard II. A headless skeleton found in the grounds is believed to have been that of the founder, who was beheaded about 1412 and his body reputedly buried at Mount Grace.

The new foundation was licensed in 1398. The Priory had a comparatively short and relatively peaceful life. The Prior and Convent, on surrendering the house quietly to the King in December, 1539, were granted pensions. What remains, after passing through private and generally caring hounds, came to the National Trust in 1953.

I crossed the outer court to the ruins of a quiet small church – ruins dominated by a tower that is familiar to Yorkshire folk through photographs reproduced in magazines and on calendars. A middle-aged couple from Teesside said: "We've passed Mount Grace, now and again, for over fifty years. Today, my wife said: 'Dad – we must go and look at it!' We'll certainly come again!"

I was fascinated by the distinctive life of the monks at Mount Grace. Not for them the notion of a disciplined life in common. Each member of the Carthusian Order was provided with a cell and spent most of his time here. But what a cell! This was no chamber cut from rock or a natural cave from which any lurking wild beasts had been evicted. It was, in effect, a small house with an adjacent garden.

A stressful executive, having toured the cool, clear rooms of a cell which exists complete, to illustrate the old way of life, said: "I wouldn't mind having a spell in that place myself. I bet there was a waiting list for accommodation here in the Middle Ages."

I saw a plain but attractive stone building with a ridged roof made of pantiles. At one end of the ridge was a stone cross and at the other end a small, ornate chimney. It is, of course, a reconstruction, prosaically known as Cell 8. The door was set in a windowless wall and the only other aperture, to the right of the door, was a serving hatch with a right-angle bend in the thickness of the wall for the delivery of food and so that there was no eye contact between the server and the inmate of the cell.

The ground floor was split into rooms. In the living room was a fireplace, table, chair and the monastic equivalent of a sideboard. Elsewhere was a chapel, also serving as a bedroom, and a study. The guide book noted that "the upper floor appears to have been used as a workshop." It was spacious, equipped with spinning wheel and handloom.

The stone-built spring-house received water from one of the many sources on the hill to the east. Charterhouses, like the houses of friars, were sophisticated in the methods devised for supplying water and conducting waste water from the precincts. An ancient leather drinking vessel was found near the well.

The addition of a harmless green dye to the water indicated that it flowed beneath the Priory and emerged at the Lily Pond. Needless to say, the water was credited with having miraculous powers.

(1991)

Dallowgill: Where the Bonnie Heather Blooms

Dallowgill Moor, of 10,000 acres, extending from 700 ft to 1,200 ft, is broad and rounded in shape – like a giant hoofmark on the Pennines east of Nidderdale. The "gill" of the name extends up the middle, dividing the moorland into two parts.

Tommy Guy, the head gamekeeper, described the ground at Dallowgill as sandy or loamy. "We can burn old heather in spring and the new growth has struck by summer."

Dallowgill is a form of double name, "dallow" itself meaning a dale. A Scandinavian origin is presumed. There is no historic nucleated village, no centre – just a scattering of farms. The school, church, chapel and what became the post office were built close together in the nineteenth century.

I went to Dallowgill in "chancy" weather. Then someone turned on a celestial hosepipe. Tatters of cloud moved aimlessly about the high ground. Rain fell on the car roof with a noisy persistency. The conditions did not deter the military jets. Half a dozen aircraft banked, circled and flew so low I fancied that one or two would return to base with bits of ling and peat on their wing-tips.

Tommy Guy and I waited for the sound waves to abate. Then I asked: "Do low-flying jets upset the grouse." Tommy replied: "No, they're used to it."

Dallowgill is a "black moor" and a hard one for sheep. It was hard on the men who trudged five or six miles across the moor to work on the construction of Leighton reservoir. If it was raining, they had no work and no pay. Dallowgill is deep and steep-sided, with some blocks of upstart conifers lower down and relict oaks higher up.

In a broad part of the gill stands the cluster of nineteenth century buildings. An Anglican church is one of nine in the district that are administered by two clergymen. The Methodist Chapel has a symbolically skyline situation.

Dallowgill has "a tight community of people." The enemy here is not the king's enemy but the weather. Farmers have a hard old fight against the elements. Older people recall the endless hard work and old-time poverty. "Conditions are not too bad now . . ."

A long tradition of comradeship is based largely on life at the chapel. "It remains very much a living force in the community." The Wesley Guild meets fortnightly in the winter in the chapel schoolroom, "where there's an enormous stove they heat up to cherry-red. If the wind's in the wrong direction, and the chimney smokes, they meet in the sitting room of a local house."

I parked outside Tom Corner Farm, which at 900 feet is just across the road from the moor, with its heather, bilberry, bracken and sphagnum moss. John Eric Spence told me his family moved to this farm in 1924.

For the first eight years they combined small-scale farming with inn-keeping. Old Ordnance maps indicate The Shooters' Inn and long after the licence was given up in 1932 people called here for refreshment. The family had not the heart to take down the old sign.

Moor-edge farming has never been very profitable. The Spences took over only 10 acres, acquiring four more, then slowly absorbing the land of three other farms, one of them occupied by Peter Kendall and still referred to locally as Old Pete's.

The herds of Shorthorn cattle suffered badly between the wars when hard-up farmers tended to use "any old scrub bulls" on their cows, resulting in a loss of quality. Today, Friesian cattle graze on new-seeded land which is well-fed with fertilisers. "It's hungry land; if you don't feed it, then it soon goes back to heather."

When John Spence left school, he sometimes went grouse-driving on the moor for 5s (25p) a day. The Vyners of Studley owned the sporting rights and the word of the head gamekeeper was law. "If a man fell out with him, the gamekeeper would say to the landlord he thought it was time *that* man was going. And *that* man had to go!"

Sheep occupy the moors by the right of a thousand generations. They are of the Swaledale breed – "Swardles" in the local parlance. Because they are inclined to seek out the lower part of the moor, which is sheltered and has the best grazing, a shepherd regularly "dogs" them to higher ground. "Otherwise," said the farmer, "they'd eat out the bottom of the moor."

Kathleen Bumstead, who lives at 200-year-old Dalton Lodge – the highest inhabited building at Dallowgill – speaks with admiration of the endurance shown by the moorland sheep. The ewes are good mothers, yet "I've known so-called springtimes when the lambs were born deep in snow and the mothers had no milk for them. I wanted to open the door and let them all in!"

Dalton Lodge bears the date 1786. Local legend has it that a man who loved grouse-shooting was put off by the exhorbitant prices charged by the inn-keeper at Kirkby Malzeard, so he built himself this lodge. All I know is that in the census of 1851, the people living here had lately come from Lamb Close (now ruined). Dalton Lodge was then a farm. It continued so for a long time. The land was absorbed in the surrounding farms and it became a keeper's cottage.

Dallowgill's high-lying acres were being enclosed by drystone walls from 1799. Last century, the population was much higher than it is today and some of those who called themselves farmers had only twelve acres or so each. How could they feed a family on the income from twelve acres? The answer lies partly in the fact that they did other jobs on a part-time basis.

During my visit to Dallowgill, grouse were talking to each other across the moorland. An old chap told me that if I wanted to know what grouse tastes like, I should go on to the moor, pull up a lump o' ling – and eat it!

Kathleen Bumstead's chief impression of Dallowgill is the demanding nature of the land. "The people have always had to work hard up here . . . You learn that nature is hard, unrelenting, cruel; you live or you die!

She added: "The stoicism, both of the people and the animals, is wholly admirable."

(1986)

Ripley: A Village with a French Flavour

Threstle his village, between Harrogate and Ripon, is self-evidently an estate village, as pretty as any village in Yorkshire and – with its cross and stocks, its cobblestones and general olde-worldiness – much in demand by television companies who are anxious to evoke the rural past.

Sir Thomas Ingilby says: "The television aerials tend to go up and down on elastic . . . We have so many layers of paint on the castle windows we can barely open any of them."

Ripley is probably derived from "ripa lea", meaning "the field by the banks of the river", indicating the first settlement's position by the River Nidd and Newton Beck. Medieval Ripley, straddling some important trade routes, also benefited from being roughly half-way between London and Edinburgh. It was a staging post for long-distance traffic, the precursers of motor coach and juggernaut lorry.

Ripley is now by-passed, but the strategic value of the area is evidenced by two roundabouts and a profusion of road-ends. The rumble of traffic is heard distantly. Harrogate and Ripon are not far away, but Ripley is neither a suburb nor a commuter's village. It is an entity, almost all of it belonging to the Ingilby family, who became landowners 640 years ago.

Sir Thomas, aged twenty-eight, showed me early copies of a monthly news sheet, *Ripley Castle Chronicle*, he had founded and was editing with considerable honesty and a distinct lack of pretention. He also gave me a potted history of his family, who had come across the Channel with the Normans "and after one or two stops they settled in Cleveland."

An Ingilby son married an heiress living at Ripley; in due course the fortified gatehouse appeared as a refuge for local people and stock when the Scots were on the rampage. As Sir Thomas put it: "They were a barbaric lot in those days, and having no Rangers nor Celtic football team to support they used to come down here every year and beat the whole place up.

"They laid waste all the villages. They carried off the cattle and the women." Sir Thomas [then a bachelor] smiled in anticipation of his next point, putting it firmly in the category of humour: "We didn't mind losing the women, but some of the cattle were a little too good for the Scots."

The village is like no other place in Yorkshire, having been built of good Yorkshire stone, and well slated, but with a distinctly French style of architecture. Sir Thomas explained that "towards the end of the eighteenth century, the village was in a bad state of repair. Sir William Amcotts Ingilby might have pulled the houses down and replaced them one by one.

"Instead, he visited France, saw a village in Alsace-Lorraine which

Cross and Stocks at Ripley (Alec Wright)

The Ingilbys of Ripley, near Harrogate, preside over a village which one of their forebears built on the lines of a village he had admired during a visit to France. Look also for a wild boar in stone. The park holds fallow deer and a host of Canada geese.

interested him, came back to Ripley, demolished the whole lot, and re-built using that French village as a model. We have lovely terraces of French houses and because they are all built of Yorkshire stone they blend in very nicely . . . If I ever got so wealthy that I could afford to stonewash all the houses, the village would turn into the most lovely golden colour."

Sir Thomas described the Town Hall, built in 1854, as "this huge Victorian gothic monstrosity". Carved in stone across the front is the proud inscription "Hotel de Ville".

Ripley is a destination in itself. The Castle and Gardens are popular with visitors. Many more, having parked their cars on the cobblestones, admire the cross and stocks, and have their photographs taken beside a carved stone boar, a feature of the Ingilby family crest. When Edward III was hunting in the Forest of Knaresborough, and his life was threatened by an injured boar, Thomas Ingilby was at hand to despatch it. He saved the king from injury and was rewarded with a knighthood.

It was way back in the 1960s that Ripley first heard the crack of the clapperboard and the shouted call for "action" as television cameras began to roll. A Yorkshire Television children's series, *The Flaxton Boys*, was filmed at Ripley, in and around the castle, over a spell of three years.

A French crew used Ripley as the setting for a film about the Brontës. "Last year," said Sir Thomas, "it was used for part of the series about No. 10 Downing Street. We had Queen Victoria and Disraeli here at the same time . . ."

My own favourite Ripley-based production was *Brother to the Ox*, using the farming recollections of Fred Kitchen. A hiring fair was created at Ripley. Sir Thomas recalled: "It went down very well with the villagers because they got parts as local drovers and children dressed up as village urchins. They based a lot of the scenes on photographs which are still in the possession of village people. It was completely authentic."

I viewed the castle from near a cascade which, connected to a generator, provides most of the electrical power for lighting the castle. "We also supply the castle and whole village with water." A wrought iron bridge was designed by Telford in 1840.

Fallow deer adorn the Park, as they have done since before the big lakes were dug out by hand in about 1844. Previously, a small stream flowed down the centre of a boggy valley. An Ingilby wife discovered Capability Brown's plans for the landscaping of the estate and she realised that there should have been lakes. For reasons of expense, these had not been created.

Sir Thomas related that she went away on holiday, after announcing that if the lakes had not been excavated by the time the holiday was over, she would not return. Her husband got an estimate of £2,500 for digging out sufficient earth to impound over 20 acres of water.

The bill came to £3,000. He was furious. There was very nearly a divorce case over it!

(1983)

Middleham: Hundreds of Racehorses

T he Wensleydale village of Middleham lives mainly by horse-racing. There's a hierarchy based on a person's relationship to the Turf. "Here it's racing first, farming second," I was told by a shopkeeper, who added: "We probably have more Irishmen than Yorkshiremen."

At the approach of the flat racing season, local people have a quicker step than at other times. Jackets come off. Sleeves are rolled up. The newspaper and television people begin to arrive. You can feel excitement in the air.

Middleham, one of two principal northern centres where racehorses are trained (the other being Malton) is well-placed, being half way from coast to coast, 180 miles from Ayr and 230 miles from Ascot. The principal courses attended by Middleham-trained horses are York, Doncaster and Newcastle.

The bloodstock to be found in and around Middleham was commended to Henry VIII in 1537. Arthur D'Arcy informed the king: "For assuredly, the breed of Jervaulx for horses was the tried breed of the North, the stallions and mares so well sorted that I think in no realm should we find

Weathered Cross at Middleham (E. Jeffrey)

The churches of Middleham and Giggleswick are under the patronage of St Alkelda, who is said to have been put to death by strangulation. The murder was committed by a heathen woman, and the incident is graphically shown in stained glass in each building. At Middleham, strings of racehorses which are stabled in the village may be seen going to and from their exercise grounds.

the like of them, for there are high and large grounds for the summer, and low grounds to serve them."

Today the area has two distinct groups of racing stables, one in the village and one a little to the north. In between is the unfenced Middleham Low Moor (365 acres), where racehorses are exercised and trained in winter. The summer gallop is the High Moor (187 acres), some springy ground at the foot of Penhill. Both tracts of ground are owned by the parish council, which leases them to a trainers' committee.

A trainer told me: "The moors are good, healthy places on which to train a horse and the best place in the world to train jumpers. Horses are rather like people. They get sick of the same thing day after day . . ." A visit to the High Moor from the village, plus training time, takes an hour and forty minutes.

More "flat" horses than jumpers are trained at Middleham and training is fast work, with the horses cantering at twenty miles an hour and reaching from thirty to thirty-five miles an hour at the gallop. Racehorses range in height from 15.2 to 17 hands and are to the average horse what a Rolls Royce is to the family saloon car.

Into Middleham comes the finest of food for the horses – both Scots and Australian oats, plus hay made from seed grass grown and harvested in the East Riding. The hay is kept for nine months before being fed.

For about £17 a week, a stable lad may be called upon to look after three horses whose collective value is possibly £30,000. Jockeys begin as lads, and to be a jockey is one of the prime incentives among those who start in the stables, though only one in five hundred apprentice jockeys will make the grade.

Some of the lads "live in", while others lodge in village homes. Yet more find quarters at the four inns. "The lads haven't much to do in their spare time. They are kept busy and are away racing quite a bit. They watch television, or go to the pubs to play dominoes and darts."

Irish boys attend the Catholic church at Cover Bridge on a Sunday." Churchgoing is not the strict affair it was in the days of trainer Dick Peacock's grandfather, who was a churchwarden. All the apprentices had to attend services."

"Swanks" Smith, aged 79, was one of the men who told me about "the old days". He was paid £4 for the first year of his apprenticeship "and if I wanted any clothes or other necessities I went to the office for a line [a chit taken to the shops which were under contract to the stables]."

The working day began at 6 a.m., though in summertime he was often out exercising horses at 5 a.m. "to beat the flies on High Moor." As a jockey, he got £3 a ride, and one way in which a jockey could lose weight quickly was to be put in a dung heap to sweat off the fat.

This Wensleydale town, so full of character, has a cosmopolitan out-look and a passion for bloodstock which must be second only to that at Newmarket.   (1971)

Hawes: Capital of the Upper Dale

Hawes is a friendly town, until you invoke the wrath of the native by calling it a village. (A similar explosive response may be noted at nearby Dent). Hawes is not very large, nor is it very old.

All this might give the impression that Hawes is a village, but then it is pointed out that the place acquired a market charter in 1699. The Tuesday market keeps up the old tradition.

In any case, Hawes has the *feel* of a town.

Hawes, the Capital of Upper Wensleydale, is a point of convergence for families living over a wide area. Why, there's even a movement of people over t'Buttertubs Pass from Swaledale who find Hawes is much more handily placed for them than is the market town of Richmond.

Hawes Church, Wensleydale (Frank Armstrong)

This is the only Church to stand alongside the 250-mile-long Pennine Way footpath. Travellers heading north use a flagged way, with a few "welly gates", the hinges being composed of the soles of redundant wellington boots.
The Tuesday Market, with its roadside stalls, gives Hawes a carnival atmosphere. There is non-stop variety when a sheep sale is being held at the busy auction mart.

Hawes has a linear appearance, between fellside and riverside flats. Look at a map and you will discover that the nearest places of importance – Kirkby Stephen, Sedbergh, Leyburn and Ingleton – are rather more than sixteen miles from Hawes, which is good for the town. It gives it a chance to develop its own character. Like an American frontier town, Hawes – virtually a one-street place, but without hitching posts for horses – has a true community, self-reliant and neighbourly.

The tourist at Hawes is spoilt for choice. Here are four pubs, cafes, a host of shops and a scattering of toilets. I have sometimes begun a long summer's day with coffee in Hawes and, returning by way of the town in the gloaming, buying some of the celebrated fish and chips before resuming the journey through Widdale to Ingleton.

Hawes, though it is "hawf way across t'country", has a sea fishing club. Being so far from either coast, its members can travel west or east depending on mood and weather forecast. Hawes, at an elevation of 850 ft., is said to be named from the Norse *hals*, signifying a pass between mountains.

Being hemmed in by the Pennines, the folk of Hawes have a speech more closely related to the eastern region than to the west. If you are chilled in Dent, you're "carled", whereas in Hawes you are "cawld". Subtle differences occur in the dialect of Old Hawes (Norse) and Askrigg (Danish). The two places are a few miles apart. Emergency medical cases are taken to hospital at Northallerton, which is "knocking forty mile away".

Hawes shop-keepers do not seem to have developed a commercial rivalry; they help each other out. One visitor noticed "a lot of to-ing and fro-ing . . . I called at one shop. When the owner hadn't got what I wanted, he slipped out and got it for me – from a shop lower down the street." The smell of home-baked bread is carried through the town on the early morning breeze.

Hawes has two major enterprises, each a source of considerable pride – the Creamery and the Auction Mart. Wensleydale cheese-making began as a farmhouse occupation and then was conducted by the Chapmans in an old mill powered by Gayle Beck.

Kit Calvert, Dalesman extraordinary, ran the cheese enterprise from the late 1920s to 1966, during which time the premises standing just off the road to Gayle were purpose-built. [Since this article was written, the Creamery was closed down. Happily, cheese-making has now been resumed.]

Hawes Auction Mart Company is undoubtedly a success story. At the verge of living memory are the days when stock stood or was penned in the main street and when farmers, carrying gold coins rather than cheque books, tended to be "bow-legged wi' brass". The mart was built and periodically extended. In 1982, the sales turnover was an awesome £8,655,000.

The old Market Hall, built in Victorian times, and controlled by the Charity Commissioners, is to be transformed into a community centre.

I shall be sorry to lose the atmosphere of the old hall, which was set up with money left by a man who specified there should be no smoking, no drinking and performances which, on the Sabbath, were restricted to sacred music. Efforts to run bingo at the hall were easily defeated by the diehards.

I have a special remembrance of the cafe. A farm man entered. One of the lady helpers asked him what he wanted. "What's tha got?" The helper suggested beans on toast. The farm man reflected for a moment or two, then replied: "Aw reet – if tha hasn't getten any plates."

(1983)

Aldwark: Where you Pay to Cross the River

The Aldwark Toll Bridge, over the Ouse, to the north of York, has twenty-seven arches and culverts, five of which are of wood. It spans a river which runs fast and deep in a sound-proofed bed of sand and mud, draining a quarter of Yorkshire.

It was misty in the Plain of York. A local shopkeeper said: "It'll clear when t'daylight goes." I turned towards Aldwark, first paying 8p at the Toll Bridge, which was being manned by Betty and Frank Clark.

Frank invited me to tour the Toll House, which has white exterior walls and is roofed by red pantiles. Inside was quite a large kitchen, a relatively small bedroom, a bathroom and a sizeable living room, being an extension of the original building. A simple porch, with glass panes, ensures good visibility up and down the road and enables the Keepers of Aldwark Bridge to cheat the wind and rain.

The Clarks are on duty for ten hours a day. The weight limit for vehicles is eight tons. Long before the Ouse was spanned, the Romans had a ferry. Their stone landing place was re-discovered in recent times. Then a wooden bridge enabled travellers to cross dryshod.

This bridge collapsed in the middle of last century. It was winter-time and ice floes were being carried along by the force of the water. Fourteen children were among those watching the passage of the floes. The youngsters had suddenly moved from one side of the bridge to the other. Coincidentally, a lump of ice struck the bridge, causing it to collapse. The children were tossed into the water and drowned. Only one body was recovered.

In a serious flood, some twenty years ago, the boat kept at Dunsforth to ferry anglers across the river broke loose from its chain and made an unscheduled voyage. The boat crashed into the Toll bridge and damaged it. At the same time, a hen hut floated downriver, with some attendant cockerels perched on the roof and still having enough spirit to crow. Though swept clear of the bridge supports, the hut sank in the deeps beyond.

Alan Ellis, when young, saw a lad from Ouseburn dive off the top rail of the bridge into the river. "He did it in summer; it's a long way down."

Little commercial traffic is seen on the river today. Pleasure craft are in the ascendancy. Well over 500 boats may be moored above Linton Lock in summer. A scattering of canoes originates at a Boy Scout centre near the Toll Bridge.

The village of Aldwark, built of brick and red pantile, looks at first glance to be a quiet little estate village where "time stands still". Yet this is a community with its sleeves rolled up.

The farms lie within the area of the village. Lorries collect loads of potatoes or sugar beet. The cattle are beef animals and the sheep are heftier than the little dark-faced, horned sheep of the Dales. The human population of less than 200 is outnumbered by farm stock.

Nearby Linton-on-Ouse sends its jet aircraft zooming across country and so the villages are inclined to be noisy. When lines were drawn on a map to indicate the area with the highest decibel level, only one house at Aldwark lay within it, which is a pity, for then there would have been free double-glazing for its houses.

Aldwark Church is distinctive, its main walls being built of pebble-rubble and bricks. The bricks were laid in diagonal or herringbone courses. Limestone for windows, arches and mouldings were brought from West Hartlepool.

The old Aldwark Estate was split up for sale in 1947, when wartime memories were fresh. Canadian airmen had been billeted at Aldwark Hall. The drone of outgoing bombers was to be heard at night as aircraft left the local airfields. Aldwark Toll Bridge was strengthened so that it could handle the passage of Army tanks.

I used Aldwark toll bridge again when resuming my journey to York. The mist dispersed from the Vale, as the shopkeeper foretold.

(1991)

Lead: The Ramblers' Chapel

E ngland has many "lost" villages with only a church to remind us of their previous existence. This is the case at Lead. The old manor house and attendant buildings have gone but the isolated private chapel of the most influential local family endures.

Lady Clegg, of Saxton, south of Tadcaster, told me about the Friends of Lead Church and an annual service held each May. "It is sometimes known as the Ramblers' Church," she wrote. "It stands alone in a field.

Ramblers and cyclists have met there in the past and they helped to restore it in 1934."

From Saxton to Lead by road took little more than five minutes. Then Lead Chapel came into view, being limestone-grey and gleaming because the sunlight was upon it and the sky beyond had a contrasting storm-blackness.

The place was rendered as Lied in the Domesday Book, at which time "Gunner had two carcutes to be taxed and there may be three ploughs there . . ." Values had increased, the place being worth 20 shillings in King Edward's time and in 1086, the time of the Domesday Survey, no less than 30 shillings.

St Mary's endures among the daisies and the cow-pats. The road verge near The Crooked Billet inn had been flattened to concrete-hardness by the pilgrims' cars. This pilgrimage was not arduous, involving crossing the road and a bridge over Cock Beck. Beyond lay a wooden stile. I then took a diagonal course across a field to where the building stands in grand isolation.

There was time to pause near the beck which, after the Battle of Towton, in the 15th century, is said to have run red with blood. I bowed my head for most of the way across the field, not because I was feeling penitent but because the field was littered with fresh sheep droppings.

Lady Clegg had mentioned that Lead was, until 1912, a detached part of the parish of Ryther. The chapel was probably associated with the manor house, about which little is known. An outcrop of masonry between the Chapel and Lead Farm may be what remains of a medieval hall.

I heard the rumble of traffic on the Great North Road and the whine of military aircraft. At harvest time, combine harvesters lumber across this fertile district like antedeluvian monsters, gorging themselves on grain and leaving trails of straw which another metallic monster winds into enormous rolls. The area is strung about by pylons and wires, for not far away are the cooling towers of the power station which provides a stupendous backdrop to Fairburn Ings.

As I approached Lead Chapel, using one of the shortest public footpaths in Yorkshire, I was impressed by the stoutness of the walls and the soundness of the roof. It has a bell in a small tower to call the faithful to worship. The stone windows are a matching set. Some itinerant stonemasons would work here to a grand design.

The pasture on which I strode might have been sheep land for over a thousand years and at the field boundaries are ancient trees, the remnants perhaps of an old forest known to Robin Hood, who some claim to be a Yorkshireman.

A wooden barrier protects the chapel doorway from rubbing by sheep; they rub themselves on the barrier instead. Some years ago, cows entered the building, causing a mess which was cleaned up using water carried across the field from Cock Beck.

At Lead Church, a visitor is like an intruder into the eighteenth century, with some evidence of much earlier times. Such is the peacefulness within this solitary building. The walls are thick enough to muffle even the bleating of sheep. I felt I could have happily stayed there forever!

A three-decker pulpit is of eighteenth century date. Near it are medieval benches, crude in their construction, fastened together in two blocks, one at each side, and having a dry, grey, unpolished appearance, almost as though they had been fashioned from driftwood. Pieces of wood hanging from the walls are adorned by religious homilies. Two of the wooden decorations are from old roof bosses and were originally gilded.

A leaflet published on behalf of the Redundant Churches Fund, which now cares for the building, mentions the Tyas family from the Low Countries who in the twelfth century were at Lead as tenants of the de Lacy family. The Tyas coat of arms featuring three mallets is conspicuous on tombs in the old chapel, tombs dating back to the eleventh century.

In due course, the Scargill family inherited Lead and when this line had run its course, about 1530, the estate passed to the Gascoignes of Parlington, who held it until recent times. In 1650, when there was no minister here, a Parliamentary Commission recommended the annexation of Lead to Saxton parish, but Lead maintained its independence.

Among its good friends today, apart from the Ramblers and the Redundant Churches Fund, is the Richard III Society, hence the presence of a wild boar in stained glass on the window behind the altar.

The most astonishing facts about Lead Chapel are, as the leaflet writer declares, its apparent simplicity, its isolation – and its survival.

(1989)

Hoyland: Once ringed by Collieries

This hill town between Barnsley and Sheffield sprang into industrial prominence mainly through mining. Its good fortune in Victorian times was that it lay near seams of quality coal. A pall of smoke testified to any passing coal owner that all was well with the world.

The New Year at Hoyland was welcomed not only by the sweet sound of church bells but by the wailing of colliery buzzers. Normally, a buzzer announced the start of a shift. For many years, a chorus of buzzers cut through the frosty air at the stroke of midnight.

A watchnight service was held at a local church. Afterwards, the young folk of the congregation toured the town, stopping outside selected houses and singing the hymn "Sweet is the Work" to the tune *Deep Harmony*. Hoyland's own band toured the town playing "Hail Smiling Morn".

Margaret Ottley, the local historian, told me that nowadays "there are no late night noises". Margaret's book, *While Martha Tolled the Hours*, is a graphic account of life at Hoyland mainly during her childhood and adolescence.

Martha was the clock on the Town Hall. The brave new Hoyland of the 1970s had no place for this Victorian building, which was demolished, the site now occupied by a supermarket, over which are the new Council offices. Martha – the old civic clock – is at present in storage with a celebrated clock-making firm, Potts of Leeds.

I visited Hoyland on a cloudless day in July. The gardens and some of the road verges held the glory of roses in full bloom. I will long remember those roses. Their exceptional quality may come from some lingering trace in the soil of the soot which accumulated during the industrial period.

A hush had descended on Hoyland that Wednesday afternoon. The main street was like some mid-western town before a gun fight. A strike by NALGO had emptied the Council Offices, grandly known as the Town Hall, of its staff. Half-day closing had emptied almost all the shops.

I photographed the sign "Town Hall" hoping that the women who were sitting on a nearby seat would not notice the camera and act naturally. I had not taken into account the friendliness of local folk.

A shrill voice startled even the migrant pigeons: "Make sure you've got us good sides!" There is about Hoyland speech something of the quality of the native tongue in a D H Lawrence novel – the clipped words, the short a's and a dropping of aitches.

A small, wheezy man with a sad expression on his face told me that he had been made redundant at a local coal mine – 20 years before! A most determined man, with two sticks, walked slowly up a hill and paused sufficiently long to tell me that "t'doctor wanted me to have a wheelchair. I told him he could keep it. I'll walk as long as I can..." Such is the spirit of the old 'uns at Hoyland.

Hoy is a Norse or Danish word meaning "hill" or "hill-land". Hoyland Common has not been common land in the open, skylarky sense since the nineteenth century when, with the opening of more collieries, streets of houses were built there as homes for immigrant workers.

Margaret was born and still lives in Netherfield House, which was built by Dr William Smith Booth. The house is of local yellow sandstone, with woodwork of high quality made, so it is said, by a craftsman who was working off a medical debt.

The South Yorkshire landscape is one of contrasts – between fields of wheat and barley and slagheaps, most of which have now been levelled and seeded with grass. As Margaret showed me around the area, she delighted in pointing out sylvan settings, with cows grazing up to their hocks in good grass and woodland round about. The trees are not upstart conifers but a natural mix of indigenous species, with lots of ash.

At Elsecar, what had been a railway in a cutting was now simply a cutting, half clogged with trees. The canal, which was closed in the 1920s, is now an elongated pool, on the banks of which grow a variety of wild flowers, from dog-daises (once known hereabouts as moon-pennies) to rosebay willow herb.

It is becoming increasingly difficult for a stranger to pick out the places where the collieries stood. Margaret Ottley, as a child, saw miners returning home after work. They were in their "pit muck", being black and grimy with coal dust. It was the period before pithead baths had been installed.

The Hoylanders bought their coal loose, a ton at a time. It was delivered by horse and cart and tipped outside the houses. The householder had to shovel coal into the cellar. "Everyone could afford to have a roaring fire and all this smoke and dirt went out into the atmosphere."

Our mini-tour of the Hoyland area ended at Tankersley, near the old church, the woods, the golf course – and the ever-busy M.1. Tankersley is in essence a delectable spot, yet this day we heard the incessant traffic roar.

Said Margaret: "I don't know how the dead manage to sleep in Tankersley Churchyard. It must be very trying for them at times . . ."

(1990)

A GLEAM OF WATER

Aysgarth: Cataracts of the Ure

Wensleydale is broad, with a major road on each side and the River Ure somewhere in between. Even at Aysgarth, it is necessary to turn into a byroad to find the river. Now the Ure is seen at its liveliest. White with fury, it pours over limestone ledges for a mile and a-half, during which the river descends for a total of over 100 feet in a tree-rimmed gorge.

At Aysgarth, the river has its last wild fling in the upper dale before making sedate progress through the park-like scenery of the lower valley. The popularity of Aysgarth Falls has been acknowledged by the road authority, who have bestowed their major award: double yellow lines.

Aysgarth and its tumbling water form one of the Dales "honeypots". The Upper Falls are the handiest. Park the car (at a small charge) and

A Waterfall at Aysgarth (Karl Stedman)

With a flight of three attractive falls, Aysgarth has become one of the Dales "honeypots", with cafes, information centre and car parks. Bishop Pococke, an early tourist, favourably compared the effect of the Ure's flow over the horizontally-bedded rocks with the cataracts of the Nile.

walk down a path with a durable surface and before long you hear the boom of water. Walk for another few yards, and you emerge from woodland cover, blinking at the light, half closing your eyes against the gleam of sunlit water.

The Middle Fall, approached along a path which in wet weather has the consistency of Yorkshire pudding mixture, with a sporting descent to river level on the exposed roots of trees, looks sublime after moderate rainfall. In spring and summer, the fall is viewed through a frame of leaves.

The summer sun lights up the water but the steep ground beyond remains in shadow. The slope is crowned by the silhouette of Aysgarth's massive parish church. The Lower Falls were called Aysgarth Force by the artist Turner who (wrote John Philips) had bestowed on them "some touches of his magic pencil".

Many a writer and poet attempted to describe the sensations aroused by Aysgarth's foaming river as it tumbles over the neat horizontal ledges of the Great Scar Limestone. Yet here there is no deadly uniformity. Though it would appear that the Creator worked with a ruler, and at times with a spirit level, the limestone beds impressed by their varied thicknesses.

An early visitor, Michael Drayton, called the river "the sovereign flood of the North Riding" and Aysgarth Falls the "crown and climax" of the river's course. Bishop Pococke, whose enthusiasm for anything was easily roused, preferred these Wensleydale falls to the cataracts of the Nile.

Today, the route to the Middle and Lower Falls, through Freeholders' Wood, may be tacky underfoot. I slithered along, humming part of *The Skater's Waltz*, descending to where a fall of some thirty feet was enveloped in spray. It was an easy walk to the Low Falls.

There is no close season at Aysgarth Falls. They are never dull. My own favourite season is autumn, when Freeholders' Wood beside the river wears its Joseph's coat of many colours and there is double beauty as the few calm stretches of the river, between the tumultuous cascades, pick up the hues of tinted leaves.

(1985)

Gormire: A Place of Mystery

Imagine, if you will, a circular lake ringed by trees . . . a mere raindrop of a lake situated in a hollow beneath an unstable cliff. Lake Gormire is a grand title for what is a modest feature. Park your car at the top of Sutton Bank and look out across the Plain of York. Now look downwards, and to the right. Tucked in to the base of the cliff, 500 feet below, is Gormire.

It is a strange lake in that there is no inflow stream and the overflow seeps away between boulders and a tangle of deciduous growth.

Glider near Sutton Bank (Bernard Fearnley)

The rim of the Hambleton Hills near Thirsk is a splendid launching place for gliders. The road zig-zags up Sutton Bank. Half hidden by trees is Gormire, a lake which has long been associated with mysterious happenings, though it is neither as deep nor as spooky as people have been led to suppose. No inlet stream is apparent and water seeps away in shingle.

Broad-leaved trees are massed around the water. Weed grows far out from the shore. Pike cruise in an aquatic jungle and on the water are coot and grebe.

Gormire is private and the public access is limited. Notices prohibit fishing, boating and swimming. Energetic visitors to Sutton Bank use a nature trail which involves 500 feet of descent with, of course, a similar distance of ascent after they have negotiated some level ground, with wooden boards over marshy bits.

Some visitors approach from Gormire Farm, using a steep stretch of road to a parking area near the farm, a charge being made for each vehicle (and the money going towards the cost of road maintenance).

Gormire might have been made as a romantic background for strange tales. One story relates that the Devil, while riding a white horse, tumbled from the cliff and vanished into the ground. A considerable hole slowly filled with water; hence – a lake! The White Mare of Whitestone Cliff (known locally as Wissoncliff) features in a number of tales.

Gormire, like Malham Tarn and Semerwater, originated through glacial action. Landslips blocked part of the meltwater channel below Whitestone Cliff, obstructing the drainage. Rock movements occurred in the eighteenth century and among those who wrote about them at first hand in 1755 was John Wesley.

It is believed that Gormire is sustained only by direct rainfall and by water draining from the moors. Old tales talk of endless depths, but the edges are clearly shallow and there is much weed, with some bullrushes. One story tells of a subterranean cliff.

A quarter of a century ago, the Yorkshire Underwater Research Group investigated Gormire, having read a feature in a local newspaper about this "lake of mystery and legend". There was even talk of a resident monster.

The divers did not have to dive deeply. The bed of Gormire was found to be composed of silt which, when disturbed, clouded the water. Stringy weed reached up towards the light. One member of the diving group compared the weeds to "drowned green hair". The only living thing encountered was a doleful perch playing a half-hearted game of hide and seek behind a rusty pipe.

Gormire was once much deeper. Two terraces mark earlier shorelines, one terrace being over 15 feet above the present lake level. Large rocks on the bed of Gormire may have come from the cliff fall of 1755.

I located the outflow. The water was seeping into the ground, though a local tale relates that a goose swimming on the lake entered a narrow chasm under Whitestone Cliff and disappeared. When next seen, it was featherless and at a spring near Kirkbymoorside, a dozen miles away.

At Gormire, soft sandstone was quarried and broken up as "donkey stones", which proud West Riding housewives rubbed on their doorsteps. Deer are among the inconspicuous denizens of the woods. Few people wander into an area which almost every writer has referred to as a "jewel".

This jewel has a magnificent setting.

(1986)

Hell Gill: Such a Deadly Place

This is no volcanic gash in the earth's surface, with the glow of hot embers and the wailing of a stricken people. "Hell" is from the Norse *hella*, a cave. The cave lost its roof and is now an awesome gorge. The local farmer said: "I don't know if there's any spot like it . . ."

Even if you do not know Hell Gill, you may have seen where the beck takes a leap into space at a waterfall which is within easy viewing distance of the Settle-Carlisle railway at Aisgill. What a splendid feature Hell Gill Force is when the beck has responded to heavy rain. It jumps from a lip of rock with the verve of Niagara.

Hell Gill, at the old boundary between Yorkshire and Westmorland, cradles the River Eden. Not far away is one of the principal feeders of the River Ure, a wholly Yorkshire watercourse. The local farmer, Chris Alderson, says that the area has good sheep country, with heather and mosscrops.

Jossie Atkinson and John Scarr told me about peat-cutting on these borderland mosses. Peats were laid out to dry and harden in the wind and sunshine. Then turves were reared against each other for further drying until they might be stacked in such a way that wind and sunshine could get at them.

Hell Gill farmhouse has a huge peat-house. Neville Wiseman, who bought the property after it had been derelict for many years, and separated

Waterfall in Hell Gill (Frank Armstrong)

In this area, North Yorkshire gives way to Cumbria. The gill carries the infant Eden and the waterfall is seen by travellers on the Settle-Carlisle Railway. I have enjoyed my jaunts to the stone bridge spanning the gill proper – a narrow ravine lagged with ferns. A highwayman (some say Nevison) leapt the gill to escape the constables of Old Westmorland.

from its fields, has some rights on the common – "a right to cut peat [turbary], a right to graze six sheep and a fell pony."

The bridge spanning Hell Gill is on a route used by the Romans and, in later times, by Lady Anne Clifford, while travelling by horse-drawn coach from her Yorkshire estates to those of Westmorland. There would be pedlars and packhorse traffic. At about the time of Brough Hill Fair [for horses] local people were known to erect stalls near the bridge and to sell wares to the travellers.

Dick Turpin's Leap is obscured by a heady growth of trees and grass. Locally, it is believed that the highwayman who leapt the gorge when escaping from the constables of Westmorland was a North Country man, Will Nevison.

It was time for me to wade into the mouth of the gorge, to carefully negotiate waterfalls and inch my way around quite deep pools. The water was crystal clear. Rounded pebbles at the bed of the beck had the clarity of objects lying behind a plate glass window.

Within the gorge, the air chilled; it became gloomy, though looking up I saw the sunlight had created a fantasy of twisted branches and multi-tinted leaves from the trees lining the rim of the deep ravine.

Neville Wiseman had traversed Hell Gill three times in the week before my visit. He described the experience as "stupendous". There had been a long drought, and with virtually no water it was possible to admire all the limestone formations. Neville and his companions had, none the less, to swim through a pool lying about half way along.

That early topographer, Leland, heard that "the bek cawled Hell Gill" was so named because "it runneth in such a deadly place". To Victorian writers, Hell Gill was a "Stygian rivulet".

The farmer had not traversed Hell Gill but "a lot of people went through last summer, when it was particularly dry." He was not over-awed by the prospect, commenting: "I should think it's a good cool place on a hot day."

(1985)

River Swale: Born in the Big Country

T he eye follows a succession of lean, dark ridges. Bilious green mosses lie in the hollows and there is some heather on the drier ground. Even the meadows and pastures at the edge of the moors tend to be wet and cold.

Spring is tardy. Summer may be little more than a wink before the year begins to run down again. Angram Common is the last flourish of Yorkshire, which here presses against the boundary of Cumbria.

Eden, Ure, Swale – these three great rivers have their beginnings hereabouts. Water gurgles through the beds of rushes, trickles down

Wainwath Falls, near Keld (Herbert Rodmell)

The Swale begins, like the other great Yorkshire rivers, with a seepage of water through the rush-bobs. Soon becks are formed which join together to form a powerful flow. In the early manhood of its life, the river goes white with fury as it tumbles over outcropping rock. Wainwath Force is backed visually by an imposing cliff.

rocks, forms becks in channels gouged in the fellsides and is eventually distinguished by the name of river.

The Swale is said to begin where Great Sled Dale Beck meets Birkdale Beck at Lonnin End, near Stone House. A "lonnin" is a lane. A farmer told me: "When I was a lad I used to stop on my way to the moor and look down t'shaft at Lonnin End. Over the years, I've dropped many a hundred stones into that shaft. You could see water at bottom. After a pebble went in, it was a long time afore t'bubbles stopped coming up. It must be fairish deep."

There was a bridge where the Swale begins; it served the lead mine at Lonnin End. The bridge was washed away in a big flood, about 1895. "There's stones laid in beck now where t'arch dropped; they are all in a piece."

The tones of the landscape lightened as I motored eastwards. The chocolate-brown of peat gave way to the dull greens of permanent pasture, with a few lighter patches where farmers had planned to have meadows but they lost the battle with the elements.

Sometimes the sheep belonging to neighbours were taken up [being classed as strays]. Then word was sent to the rightful owners "and they would come for 'em on t'moortop, against t'boundary, and hand 'em ower. You knew all t'farmers and shepherds from spots like Cotterdale and Hell Gill. Now they're fencing everywhere – it's all new posts and wires."

Swale is a lively river, deep-sunk, not so much rushing as tumbling for there are impressive falls: Wainwath, Catrake, East Gill, Kisdon. The scouring Swale demolished Gunnerside Bridge thrice in seven years. Ivelet Bridge endures, springing over the river in a single high arch, like a rainbow set in stone.

Much has changed. Farms have been amalgamated. At Keld, a school which had thirty names on the register had to close. The inn was closed. Percival's bus service, which had maintained three round trips a day, came to an end. The use of the hall declined. "We'd get a couple of hundred people for a whist drive, supper and dance . . ."

Of recent years, Swaledale has become renowned for the beauty of the setting and the appeal of its heritage. "A lot of Dutch people come up here. They think Swaledale's wonderful. Course, wi' all these hills, it's such a big change for 'em."

(1983)

The Wharfe: A River in a Hurry

This watercourse takes its name from a Saxon word, "guerf", meaning swift. If you doubt the lustiness of the Wharfe, visit the river an hour or two after storms have raged across the fells. The level of the river may rise from three to four feet in a couple of hours.

Joe Smith, the water bailiff on the length between Grassington and Barden, described the Wharfe as "a spate river, with a moving bottom". The appearance of its bed changes from year to year as freshets move the shingle. In dry weather, the flow is two cubic metres a second and when there is a spate, this increases to 430 cubic metres.

Records show when serious floods carried away bridges, even buildings. Once the hills were like a giant sponge, absorbing water and releasing it gradually into the becks and the river. The erosion of the once extensive areas of blanket peat by such factors as acid rain and a mis-guided inclination towards gripping [open drainage] means there is now a fast-run off.

In the past, water represented power to turn machinery. The first-known mill to harness the flow of the Upper Wharfe is believed to have been constructed at Kettlewell in the early thirteenth century, for the grinding of corn.

This river passes through outstanding limestone scenery. Rock and sward produce a patchwork of white and emerald green. The unpolluted state of the river, says Joe, is in part due to the influence of the anglers, who have striven to keep a clear, cool river.

The Wharfe, which begins with a blending of two becks at Beckermonds, surges down Langstrothdale, flows between Hubberholme Church and the George Inn, and enters the main valley around Buckden. Near where the Skirfare joins the Wharfe is the sphinx-like Kilnsey Crag.

Kilnsey Estates founded a fish farm, presided over by Joe Pope. Many of the rainbow trout reared here end their days on the plates of diners at hotels and restaurants over a wide area. I watched Joe hurl food pellets into water which seemed to boil as hundreds of trout tussled for their lunch. Elsewhere, fish weighing up to about 4 lb cruised in clear water, where they resembled mini-submarines.

Bolton Priory, beside the Wharfe (Janet Rawlins)

The Wharfe, which begins with a merger of becks at the well-named Beckermonds, becomes turbulent at the Ghaistrills and Strid. By the time Bolton Abbey is reached, it has regained its composure. An Augustinian priory stood at Bolton. Now that the river footbridge has been renovated, and a concrete sill provided, the famous stepping stones are invariably under water and the ruins of the Priory frequently reflected in the river.

Anglers venerate the brown trout of the Wharfe (notice how so many big fish end up "stuffed" in glass-fronted cases) and about seventy per cent of the angling is done with wet flies. The river trout run to a pound or one and a-half pounds, though Joe Smith, the water bailiff, had seen a Wharfe trout which made the scales dip at 14 lb.

A river trout's neighbours includes shoals of grayling and crayfish, which have been called "freshwater lobsters".

Water from the Wharfe, stored in Chelker reservoir, eventually gushes from urban taps. At the time of my visit Grimwith reservoir, on a tributary of the Wharfe, was being enlarged so that in dry weather it might augment the flow of the river, the required water being then abstracted several miles away for the benefit of Bradford and its satellite towns and villages.

I was conducted round the Lob Wood river intake and pumping station where, in needy times, using vertical spindle, trunk-slung pumps, part of the Wharfe's flow may be sent up the hill to Chelker reservoir, where the water is blended with that from the Barden resources. A pumping station at Chelker forwards the mixed water to Bradford, for treatment at Chellow Heights.

The song of the Wharfe is generally a pleasant song. The noise level at Lob Wood in time of drought would be intolerable if each pump motor had not been provided with a water cooled enclosure and if the building itself had not been specially designed to ensure an acceptable level of sound transmission.

Even so, the dipper, grey wagtail and other river birds will have to sing a little louder to be heard when Lob Wood is in lusty voice.

(1980)

AT HOME
IN THE DALES

Old-time Dancing

Dales dancers, who come to life in winter, are not deterred by a few flakes of snow. An old couple related to me, calmly, how they had driven home from Dent at snowtime on a road which was only the width of the Council plough.

Tosside has its regular dances. "It's out on a blooming hilltop, miles from anywhere, yet t'dances allus go off well." It was at Tosside I first met Harry Cockerill of Askrigg, a somewhat legendary accordion-player who imparts the old Dales flavour to each gathering.

Harry "plays by ear; I don't know a note o' music." His supporters are, generally, the middle-aged and elderly who are unimpressed by flashing lights and electronic wizardry. Harry told me: "My type o' dance music is just the same as it's ever been. I can't play any different." A pause. "I've

A Yorkshire Dales Dance (Ionicus)

The dance pictured here was a "posh do", the women wearing long dresses. Dalesfolk don their "best setting-off clothes" for a winter dance. A band of two or three is well-known and most of the items on the programme are "old time". It is related that during a particularly lively Palais Glide, a wooden dance hall moved on its foundations.

played t'same tunes ever since I started – and they still dance to 'em."

Dalesfolk danced wherever there was space; where they would not become "leg-locked". At Muker, the venue was an upper room flavoured by the smell of horses which were stabled beneath the dance floor.

Some farm lads living in Wensleydale made a double crossing of Buttertubs Pass by night, using cycles. "My bike was tied up with snare wire and pieces of string. I had a few snares in my pocket for running repairs in case t'bike brok down. I had a carbide lamp and it didn't hawf stink!"

Such lads demanded value for money. "If a dance didn't go on till two o'clock, we wouldn't go to it . . . It didn't matter what time I got home as long as I got into t'house afore my mum and dad got up. I've seen me take my shoes off so dad wouldn't hear me go upstairs."

At a "village hop" in Craven, a rough wooden floor was a hindrance until someone scattered a packet of Lux all over it to make it slippery. "During the first few dances, we were sneezing our heads off!" For a special "do", men wore white gloves. "We girls had programmes, and dances were booked in advance."

The kitchen was so small, the dancers went in for supper in groups of twelve. "Mother cooked a whole ham for the sandwiches . . . There were lots of home-made cakes. By the time everyone had drunk and eaten, it was getting on for one o'clock and the dance went on until two . . . Then everybody trooped out to find their floats, traps and horses. These had been left all over t'place."

For dances at Oughtershaw chairs for the band were arranged on the boards which covered a billiards table when no games were being played. Dances at Stalling Busk are still rooted in tradition. "There's a round of dominoes; then supper, and then a bit of jazz . . . There were about ten couples t'other neet. We've getten down to not so many . . ."

Harry chuckles at the remembrance of an old Army hut in Coverdale. This hut had a sloping floor, with the stove at the lowest point. Two chaps who were merry, did not make sufficient allowance for the gradient. "I remember the look of consternation on their faces as they staggered towards the stove."

Dancing used to be of secondary importance to "arm-raising exercises" at the nearest pub. "Many a dance did not start until midnight; the dancers nivver knocked off before two, and many a time it got to three. I used to fodder cows at outbarns on my way home. Aye. I didn't know if moon was going to bed or sun was getting up."

(1982)

Bartle's Village

November is the month in which to burn an effigy of Guy Fawkes, the Yorkshireman who was found loitering with intent in the cellars of Parliament. At West Witton, in Wensleydale, the effigy of a likeable rogue – Owd Bartle, the sheep stealer – is incinerated each August.

No one truly hates Guy Fawkes and when I quizzed a dozen or so people at West Witton about Bartle, they responded with something akin to affection for Bartle, though you would not think so from the way his effigy is drenched with paraffin and incinerated on a patch of open ground on the Saturday nearest to St Bartholomew's Day, which occurs on the 24th.

The date may be close to the patronal festival of the church, but this is no Christian occasion. "We have a procession. The atmosphere is so charged, it's like a pagan rite," said a native of the place. An old lady

Burning Owd Bartle in Wensleydale

A summer event at West Witton is a Yorkshire variant on the Guy Fawkes theme, though the Dales effigy is that of Bartle, a sheep stealer. He has become something of a folk hero and hundreds of people arrive to watch him being carried from place to place before being consigned to the flames.

said, unemotionally: "What do they want to go making a fuss of a sheep stealer for?"

The story of Bartle is pure folklore, with not a scrap of information to satisfy a historian. A sheep-stealer is said to have been caught in the act and was pursued from the heights of Penhill to the edge of the village, where he met his end. Could the annual re-enactment of the chase, and the sad end of Bartle, have started out (some four centuries ago) as a warning to other light-fingered folk?

I persuaded a local man to sing the doggeral associated with Owd Bartle – the poetry recited annually when an effigy is taken round the village:

> *In Penhill Craggs he tore his rags;*
> *At Hunter's Thorn he blew his horn;*
> *At Capplebank Stee he brake his knee;*
> *At Grisgill Beck he brake his neck;*
> *At Wadham's End he couldn't fend;*
> *At Grisgill End he made his end.*
>   *Shout, lads, shout.*

Pen Hill, rising to over 1,800 ft., is a fitting backcloth for a 400 year old who-done-it such as the Bartle story. "Pen Hill looks grand on a summer day," I was told. "Yet it blocks out the sun early. We have a premature dusk. It's dark and chilly here when other parts of the dale have the sunlight on them."

The summit of the Hill falls within West Witton parish, the most easterly parish in the Dales National Park. "West Witton also has the high gallop used by racehorses from the stables at Middleham. I bet you didn't know that . . ."

Reduced to its basic elements, the effigy of Bartle consists of a bag of straw, a pair of trousers, shirt and jacket, a pair of wellies "and a bit of straw twisted round for a head." Alan Harker, the man currently responsible for Bartle's annual appearance in the village, provides the effigy with a face mask and sheep's wool beard. There is also a bit of wool round the back of his neck. "We had the same plastic mask for three or four years. I've got a new one this time."

Bartle is created from unwanted garments in the back shed at Alan's home some three days before the fiery death. In this technological age, Bartle is fitted with eyes that light up. I was shown the equipment – bulbs, flex, battery and switch. Bartle then goes into hiding in somebody's garage. "He's locked up or someone might take him, just for devilment."

At 9 p.m., Bartle is carried shoulder high by Alan and his brother Robert. They are offered drinks on their way down the village. It's all a matter of tradition. "We're pretty legless by the time we get to the bottom." Now and again they stop and shout a line or two of doggerel. "When we get to t'finish, we burn him and have a bit of a sing-song – if anyone can still sing!"

Alan mentioned the enthusiasm of visitors for the Bartle-burning custom. Several hundred people gather for the walk. Sometimes they are accompanied by a television crew with camera and arc lamps.

He added: "We feel like silly blighters, walking along wi' a bag stuffed wi' straw."

(1991)

A Taste of Swaledale Cheese

The cheese melted on my tongue. A small wedge of Swaledale cheese had been offered to me by the woman who made it. I let the cheese linger in my mouth, enjoying its mellow taste, derived from milk taken from a Shorthorn which had grazed some herby pasture-land on a hill farm in Swaledale. Here was the true taste of Dales cheese.

Mrs Marjorie Longstaff and her two cows, Tiny and Blackie, were about to retire. It would be the end of a great British delicacy known simply as "Mrs Longstaff's Swaledale". A writer in *The Sunday Times* referred to her "tiny, exquisitely fresh-tasting cheeses, produced between April and October." Randolph Hodgson, proprietor of Neals Yard Dairy in Covent Garden, was reported as saying: "Mrs Longstaff's cheese is the original. It's ancient cheese."

I had met her a few weeks before, at her moor-edge farm, Deer Park, Harkerside, high above the River Swale. I stepped from the car into silence. Then grouse began to talk to each other on the sunlit moor. Silence again. Tiny, an eight-year-old red Shorthorn cow with a crumpled horn, surveyed me from over a drystone wall. The cow's companion in the pasture was Blackie, a matronly Friesian.

Mrs Longstaff acquired her knowledge of cheese-making simply by watching her mother at work stirring in the rennet, separating curds from whey and packing the curds into tin vats to be placed in a cheese press. It was a common sight in Swaledale until the creation of the Milk Marketing Board in the 1930s.

She was the fourth generation of her family to live on Harkerside, south of the river. Bleak House, the old family home, was built for her great grandfather, Francis Kendall, who was agent for the Old Gang mine. When her brother was married in 1945, Mrs Longstaff moved with her parents to Deer Park, only a field's length away. They died in the 1960s.

On the death of her brother in 1970, Mrs Longstaff and her husband obtained the tenancy of six and a-half acres of ground and began to make Swaledale cheese again. Until that time, milk from Deer Park and Bleak House had been collected daily by the milk wagon. Her husband died in 1984.

Making Cheese in a Dales Farmhouse (Brian Waters)

Wensleydale cheese is world-famous. Cheese is made in other parts of the Dales, notably Swaledale, where I tasted a sliver of cheese from a "round pound" produced in a farm kitchen. In some places, blue (skimmed) milk was used for economy. One cheese was so tough it had to be attacked with an axe! Or so they say . . .

Deer Park was revealed to me as a typical small Dales farm. A narrow gate set in the roadside wall gave access to a field path – a path through an old-established pasture where ploughshares had not been used. This land was dressed only by "muck", the traditional Pennine pick-me-up for jaded acres.

The house, sandwiched between two barns, had a generator to provide electricity for a few elemental items, but had "neither fridge nor freezer". The cheese ripened naturally in a cool room at the back of the house.

In pre-factory days, on an upper Dales farm, the night's milk was poured into a large copper cheese kettle which was kept by "t'firespot", being left overnight for the souring process to take place. The morning's milk might be added to that already in the "kettle". Some people made the cheese in the kettle.

Rennet was stirred in and then the curds were cut, stirred, the whey drained away and the curds put in a special bag which was hung up to allow more whey to drain off. Towards night, some salt was added, the quantity depending on the size of the cheese it was proposed to make. Wensleydales were usually up to 10lb in weight.

The cheese was placed under the press, where it remained overnight, then taken out. The cloth which had enveloped it was supplanted by muslin. A cheese which was to have a mould was stored low down, where the humidity was at its highest, and cheese which were to be dried fairly quickly were placed on the higher shelves.

One cheese-buyer used to say: "I'll tak every cheese that has a fur coat on it." He selected cheese with mould about an inch long. "That man knew it would be a lively cheese."

Marjorie Longstaff was fortunate in being able to watch her mother, Mary, making cheese at Bleak House. Her cheese was noted throughout the dale. In mother's time, many of the cows were milked in remote pastures during the summer, so that the meadow grass was left untrampled in the weeks before haytime.

A Swaledale cheese was given a bath in brine for some 24 hours before it was taken to the cheeseroom to dry. There was a time when rows of stalls at Richmond market were arrayed with produce brought into town by farmers' wives. They carried "butter baskets" in which they neatly packed some cheese, butter, chickens and rabbits, "anything they could make a penny out of."

Every farm in Swaledale made cheese or butter. "The cheese was sold for as little as a shilling a pound. It was the quality and the quantity that ruled the price."

I had my taste of Swaledale cheese. That cheese lingered on my tongue, melting in my mouth, imparting a mellow, herby flavour. The goodness of milk produced on the summer-bright pastures high on Harkerside had been locked up in a small wedge of cheese, which I sampled in an old farmstead.

Mrs Longstaff, daleswoman, has now retired from farming and lives with her memories in a modern house in Reeth.

(1986)

At t'Back o' Beyond

They're plucking geese i' Scotland
    And sending t'feathers here . . .
        This Dales chant was heard as flurries of snow settled on the Pennines. Snow might lie for months on end at Cosh, two and a-half miles beyond Foxup, which itself is remote, tucked away at the head of Littondale.

Early this century, the Brown family of Cosh thought nothing of walking five miles to Horton to catch a train. They drove their spare Swaledale ewes for ten miles to the market at Hawes.

One December, the snow lay at Cosh for so long there was a danger that the sheep would starve. So William Brown gathered up all 450 of them. He then mounted his pony and drove the sheep across a white landscape, looking for green fields where farmers might provide grazing for a copper or two.

The night was spent at Neils Ing, back o' Penyghent and the journey ended in the Ribble Valley next day when William Brown found quarters for a whole month at farms around Wigglesworth.

At Cosh, and other remote farms, the Dalesfolk were ever mindful of the weather. Early in 1917, a cold snap put a crust of ice over snow. One of the sheep at Cosh spent three weeks in a snow cavern it made from trampling down the snow, its breath melting an air hole. That sheep not only lived to bleat the tale but was fourteen years old when she died accidentally, having wandered into an unattended dipping tub.

Robert Brown, son of William, recalled for me that when he milked the house-cow at Cosh in winter, it was a hand operation, undertaken as he

Halton Gill, on the way to Cosh (Constance Pearson)

Go to the very head of Littondale – and then walk another mile and a half – to find Cosh, where the farmhouse has not been used by a farming family for many years. When the Brown family was there, Mrs Brown would invite the occasional walker to have a cup of tea – so that she might hear some gossip from the outside world.

sat on a three-legged stone and having light provided by a candle stuck on a "through end".

As the Pennine year waned, the Browns laid in special stores of food and John Cowan, of Halton Gill, arrived to kill the pig. John had to have a drop of whisky "or the pig would not cure properly". He and several farmers returned a day or two later to cut up the pig meat. They stayed to play cards for the rest of the long winter night. "They played whist, sometimes nap . . ."

The name Cosh, which may have originally meant a hut or hovel, was referred to in a monastic document of 1457 as "Grenefeld Coche", being then associated with Fountains Abbey. Halliwell Sutcliffe, the writer who liked a dash of romance in his work, associated Cosh with Kosh, the shepherds' huts built high in the mountains of Scandinavia – huts which "are deserted when winter sets its teeth about the heights".

When I decided to re-visit the area, a farmer at Foxup eyed me through murk and drizzle, remarking: "It were a grand day yesterda'." I walked to Cosh, with wind-blown rain on my face, during one of the longest droughts on record. A group of oystercatchers, heading to higher ground, piped shrilly as though trying to infuse some life into a dull day.

I knew that Cosh was near when I saw two large sycamore trees. The track swerved and dipped. Into view came the farmhouse, its weather-side smeared with tar to keep out the rain. Just across the track was a large ruined outbuilding and an outbarn.

Cosh has been the property of the Morphet family of High Birkwith for the past forty years; the farmhouse is being used as a Dales centre by a Yorkshire college. Early this century, the farm was tenanted by the Campbell family. It is related that Robert Campbell, who died at Arncliffe in 1955, aged 85, had lived as a hind at the remote farm some fifty years before, attending to eighteen acres of meadowland, keeping two cows, a horse and grazing 500 sheep while summering another 700.

The Brown family, who took up residence at Cosh when the Campbell family had left, used a horse and cart to collect groceries, taking in a month's supply at a time. Provision merchants from Hebden had left the goods at Foxup. Coal was used sparingly, having been carted – five hundredweights at a time – from Grassington railway station, which lay twelve miles away. The Browns dug peat to keep the home fire burning.

Richard Brown remembers when the outbuilding was complete, holding a hay "mew", tying for four cows and a box for Daisy, a dappled grey pony which "went white" with the passing of time.

Cosh had three bedrooms for a family of eight. In the living room was the customary iron fireplace, flanked by oven and water boiler; also the slopstone [sink, though without taps] and a set-boiler [used to boil the clothes on washing day]. In winter, gaps around the doors were plugged with sacking.

The fourteen acres of meadowland were "a bit rough", the roughest ground and also the gill-sides being mown by scythe. The hay was transported to the barn on a horse-drawn sled.

Each summer, when there was a flush of sweet grass, the Browns took in up to 50 cattle belonging to other farmers. "Dad even had Highland cattle from the Pratts at Hawes. Any lucrative job was sought in those days."

Time was of no account. The family attended the Gala at Skipton, crossing the five miles of moorland to Horton-in-Ribblesdale and entraining for Skipton. The journey in reverse was cheerfully tolerated at the end of the exciting summer day.

The children had a round trip of six miles to school at Halton Gill, where the schoolmistress was "well liked", arranging for wet clothes to be dried off by the stove and supervising the making of toast at dinnertime. Two of the girls from Cosh lodged at Halton Gill from Monday to Friday, but when Richard was five no lodging place was available and so his mother kept him at home until he was seven.

During a wintry spell in 1941, when Cosh was blotted out by snow, "we took five heifers to Crummock because we were getting short of hay. We couldn't open any gates and had to walk over the walls."

A wild spot, indeed. Of one occupant at Cosh, it was said: "You're nowt but a moorpowt, lad."

A Common Grazing

The cows have got out, missus!
A farmer's wife at Low Row, Swaledale, opened the house door to be confronted by an excited holidaymaker, who added: "There are cows all over the road. They're holding up the traffic!" The local lady explained that the cows were on the road not by accident but by ancient right. "It's part of Low Row Common; you'll have to get past them the best way you can."

A queue of timid townsfolk waited for the ruminating cows to move from the highway. The farm lad who came along on a small tractor wove his way between the animals and then, taking pity on the visitors, he coaxed some of the cows on to the grass. The traffic flow resumed.

The main problem as I drove to Swaledale, using a moorland road, was not farm stock but low-flying grouse. In early spring, the high moors between Askrigg and Reeth crackled with life as moorcocks established their territories.

Whitaside and Crackpot, south of the Swale, are enclosed by drystone walls. It is on the sunny side of the dale that much of the land is still held in common. This happens at Kearton, Low Row, Little Rowleth, Gunnerside and Ivelet. At the settlements of Kearton and Gunnerside, cattle grids are in place to restrict cattle to the common.

At Low Moor, David Calvert told me that his family have rights to graze cattle on the open ground. The pasturage of a cow is called a "stint" or "gait". Last summer, this family of Calverts had the right to put twenty-nine cows on the common. "We used two of my uncle's gaits, which meant we turned out thirty-one cows."

The common extends from the dale road to the edge of the moor, where the line of demarcation is a substantial drystone wall. Moorland sheep have been known to dodge round it and to descend to the best grazings. They are also "partial" to garden plants.

Alan Sunter, of Braeside, when asked about the acreage of the common promptly calculated it with regard to the maximum number of cattle allowed on it (128), a sum that must be multiplied by three, from the time-honoured assessment of three acres per cow.

Cattle are grazed from May until the autumn. Three sheep per gait are permitted here in winter. The land is rested for six weeks in spring. Geese were regarded as "stockable" but no hens were permitted because hens cannot be restrained or controlled. In the days when horses did the heavy work on the land, up to twenty might be seen grazing at Low Row. It was decreed that one horse equalled two gaits.

Alan Sunter milked cows on the common in summer. He carried the milk home in a back-can. The use of Low Row common was vital to small-time farmers.

Alan's old farm, Riddings, was typical of Swaledale farms in that it had wintering cattle spread in small groups through several byres [or outbarns], each of which had to be visited twice a day. His successor at the farm keeps cattle in just two modern buildings which are handy to the farmhouse.

Low Row is named after its position below the line of the ancient way up the dale. The cattle which settle on the road to absorb the summer sun and chew the cud have as much right to be there as you have, dear motorist. Treat them with respect.

(1989)

Letting the Poor Pasture

I resisted the temptation to go hunting for mice in the cool recesses of Hubberholme Church, a few miles from the source of the Wharfe.

These "mice" do not scutter about, being part of the woodwork which came from the Kilburn workshops of Robert Thompson in 1934. His was a distinctive species of mouse – the church mouse, *Mus musculus Thompsoni*, fixed for all time as his trademark on the oaken pews.

Hubberholme Church evolved from a little chapel in the Wildwood.

So remote was it at the Reformation that when an edict went forth from York that objects relating to the Old Faith, such as rood lofts, should be removed, no one appears to have checked to see if this had been done at Hubberholme.

The vicar (Rev. E. D. Blanchard) told me that this church was built by the Percies in those old days when "people were obliged to attend Mass before they could go off on a day's hunting. They therefore built a little chapel on the edge of Langstrothdale Chase so that they would be mounted and away as soon as the service was over!"

Hubberholme was once served by the curate of Halton Gill, at the head of Littondale, who crossed the Horse Head Pass. The Rev. Miles Wilson, in 1743, mentioned that a public service was performed once every Lord's Day in the afternoon, except in the winter quarter, when it was in the forenoon every other Sunday because of the danger and difficulty in negotiating the Pass "over very high mountains and large drifts of snow."

Hubberholme Church, by the Wharfe (Alec Wright)

Church and the George Inn, just across the river, have long been associated. Early in the New Year, the annual letting of the Poor Pasture takes place. Among my memories of Hubberholme is attending the memorial service for J. B. Priestley, who is commemorated by a plaque. His ashes were scattered in the locality.

Thomas Lindley, the best-known curate, had a white horse and a representation of man and animal appears in the Robinson Window, in Hubberholme Church. It is said that when the wardens at Hubberholme saw man and horse "break" the skyline, they rang the bell to summon local people to worship.

The George Inn, which lies just across the river from the church, was the property of the benefice. The same key is said to have opened both church and inn. The pub attained a measure of fame through notices on the doors of the outside toilets – "tups" and "yows" – and J. B. Priestley, the prolific author, a regular visitor to Hubberholme, said that in his younger days he would have enjoyed being the landlord of the place.

Was the George really a vicarage before it became an inn? The vicar thinks this idea is unlikely, "since until the Reformation the monks of Coverham took the services. The Perpetual Curate of Halton Gill officiated until Hubberholme became a parish in its own right in 1765."

The present vicarage is a late 19th century conversion of three miner's cottages. Dora Guest, who has worked on the chronology of the place, cannot find a gap to represent the time when it was home to the vicar and his family.

Church and inn are united once a year for the letting of the Poor Pasture, a sixteen-acre plot, though this is actually vested in the vicar and his wardens, not in the Church. The money, traditionally distributed among the poor of the parish, is now used to buy bags of coal for old-age pensioners at Christmas.

It's a reight good do, with farmers converging from far and wide. The vicar and his wardens form the House of Lords. The potential bidders are the House of Commons. There is much chatter, much banter, before a bid is accepted for the following twelve months. A time limit is set on the ceremony by lighting an ordinary domestic candle. When the flame goes out, no more bids are entertained.

This year, it was with a sense of shock that the bidders saw the vicar produce a huge Pascal Candle, but this was simply intended as a joke, and soon an ordinary candle was on view, its flame sending fingers of light into the far corners of the bar (the House of Commons). John Huck started the bidding with a call of £20. Interest fell away for a few hours and then livened up, until Stan Metcalfe offered a record sum of £305.

The excitement was over for another year, for Hubberholme is a place where farming usually takes a quiet, unspectacular course.

(1986)

YORKSHIRE-BY-THE-SEA

Fishing Boat with a Viking spirit

O n a flight from Stavanager to Newcastle, I beheld a sea so calm, so blue, I had a fanciful idea that I was flying upside down – and looking at the sky.

Then small fishing boats could be observed, like colourful beetles on a pond. These were cobles, the traditional in-shore craft operating between Berwick and the Humber. Clinker-built, of Norse design, a coble is at home on the short, sharp sea of the North East coastline.

Cobles drawn up at Flamborough (Frank Armstrong)

They have snug moorings at the North Landing, being protected from all but an easterly by a recess in the range of chalk cliffs. Cobles have long been used by the inshore fishermen. The few remaining boats are also available to take anglers to sea and to provide tourists with mini-cruises and a view of some immense seabird colonies.

In Norway, I had seen the *viks* or creeks from which Norse adventurers sailed to Britain. They had clinker-built craft, with dragonesque prows. The coble retains a Norse character and, though clinker-built, has relatively few planks. The lowest, apparently twisted in all directions, imparts the distinctive shape. The topmost plank turns inwards.

On a clear, sunny day, the colours of the cobles are bright and distinctive. A knowledgeable watcher on the shore can recognise individual boats. Some of the Whitby cobles made use of red and blue, predominantly "lifeboat blue", which stands out against the sea-tones.

The coble fishermen of Yorkshire have traditionally worked from an exposed beach, hence the high bow, to deflect the crashing waves when the craft is being launched or recovered. I heard of a single sailing coble which is kept at Scarborough and retains its big brown lugsail.

Salmon cobles, the smallest type, used to slip down the Esk at Whitby by the light of lamps ashore so that they might be in position as the sky began to pearl at the coming of dawn. And I have been told about forty-foot herring cobles, each with three or four men, which operated well off-shore, including the Dogger Bank.

Today, most of the Yorkshire cobles are driven by diesel engine connected to a shaft and propeller which lie in something akin to a tunnel, being protected as the boat is hauled up the beach at the end of a fishing trip. Some cobles spend their lives floating up to their waists in salt water – at Whitby, Scarborough and Bridlington.

At Flamborough and Filey a visitor sees cobles in their traditional setting, drawn up on the beach. When in use, cobles bob off a rocky shore as the men attend to "fleets" of lobster pots.

Filey is an excellent place at which to study coble anatomy. As a boat nears the shore, the large, broad rudder is lifted from the water and the boat is turned so that it lies stern-on to the beach. A tractor is connected by chains to the stern of the boat, which is floated over a pair of wheels. Now the tractor takes over for the short journey to the Coble Landing.

For twenty-nine years, Laurie Murfield of Whitby sailed (and sometimes had to row) a coble called *Good Faith*, which was owned by the legendary Dora Walker, an enthusiast for Whitby and its traditional fishing boats. Laurie told me: "I once did eighty miles in a coble while tunny fishing. I put that boat on the south end of the Dogger, where there were nine fathoms o' water."

In this technological age, the fisherman consults a radar set and is aware of the movement of other craft up to twenty-five miles away, a boon and a blessing when a roke [sea fret] "wet as a dishclout" has enveloped the area. In the old days, it was an eerie sensation to be in a coble when a roke descended. The engine was cut periodically as the fishermen listened for the *plish*, *plash* of the tide breaking on the beach.

He now moves confidently, using radar as his foul-weather eyes. A "fishfinder", working on the sonic principle, sends out sound-waves which are reflected back from shoals of fish. Some cobles have the Decca satellite navigator and, with its help, a fisherman can fix his position to within ten yards.

The traditional shape of the coble, a popular in-shore craft, conceals a range of new equipment. It's a pity that the herring, crab, lobster and salmon are now so scarce on our North East coast.

(1986)

White Walls of Yorkshire

The owner of Grange Farm at Bempton was reported to be selling thirteen acres of "rugged cliff face" and three acres of cliff-top land near Bridlington. He rightly described this property as "a unique piece of land".

Here is the seaward termination of the ridge of chalk which extends across the Wolds to end abruptly with white cliffs up to four hundred feet in height. The chalk has an overlay of boulder clay and is thatched with grass and wild flowers in great profusion.

The waves break their backs against cliffs which are cracked and seamed, holding – in spring and summer – about a hundred thousand pairs of nesting seabirds. The musky smell of guano curls over the cliff.

Indentations form echo-chambers for the growling guillemots and razorbills. The guillemots on their ledges look like rows of brown-and-white skittles. Kittiwakes, forming Europe's largest nesting colony, are everywhere. Excited birds swirl like snowflakes in a blizzard.

Flamborough Head, to the south of Bempton, has a North Landing and a South Landing. In good weather, it is outrageously colourful, the sky and sea tones, plus the white and green of the cliffs, being diversified by the multi-colours of the cobles, lying on the shingle like seals which have hauled themselves out of the water to sunbathe.

The inshore fishermen had an arrangement whereby if weather conditions changed and the boats were diverted from the North landing to the South on their return, the small son of one of them might leave school early to take the donkeys round to the South Landing, where they were needed to transport tackle and fish back to the village.

I voyaged in the coble *Prosperity*, with Richard Emmerson at the tiller and Peter Ellis in support. The boat was coaxed from a shore which in places was covered with weed and elsewhere was pebbly. Thousands of pieces of chalk, torn from the native cliffs, had been wave-licked into smooth pebbles.

Sand martins twittered as they flew around their nesting holes, which they had drilled into the soft ground between the chalk and the grass.

Kittiwakes rose from the water to form white clouds. Far out, the sea was Prussian blue; near the shore, it had a turquoise hue.

The coble, with its sturdy construction – larch on oak – was exceptionally steady. I was told that long years ago cobles were built at Whitby by "hand and eye". If I took a line down the centre, the two halves would not match up precisely, as they would in a modern coble.

We sailed on a high tide, so we hugged the coast, first entering Thornwick Bay, to the north. Here the Smugglers' Cave was so large it looked as if the cliff was yawning. As the voyage resumed, I watched the lines and chevrons of seabirds returning to the White Cliffs after feeding offshore. Puffins were working their wings so briskly, I entertained the thought that those wings might break off through bone-fatigue.

The flight of gannets was graceful and languid. On my first visits to Bempton, no gannets were nesting here. Then some birds from Bass Rock began to occupy broad ledges which had been used by guillemots. Into being came the only nesting colony of gannets on the British mainland.

We turned southwards, to enter a shallow inlet containing the pinnacle known as the Queen Rock. Once there was a King. "It's always said the King Rock collapsed about the time that George VI died. It's probably not quite true . . ."

The high cliffs were bird-busy. Guillemots adorned the ledges and stood on shelving rocks close to the sea. At our approach, the birds dived into the breaking waves and departed underwater. Kittiwakes shouted. Jackdaws chacked. Herring gulls gave laughing calls, as though responding to some doubtful jokes.

Our return to North Landing was escorted by more incoming seabirds. Ours being the last voyage of the day, the coble was hauled from the sea using wire rope and tractor power. The tractor pulled; the cable tightened and the coble ran smoothly on skids formed of baulks of timber deftly deposited before the advancing boat.

Along the cliffscape of North-East Yorkshire, where the summer sun rises and sets over the sea, a myriad seabirds flew with the sunlight upon them.

(1990)

The Land Ends at Spurn

I crossed Yorkshire diagonally, from North Ribblesdale to Holderness. At home, the sun was beginning to light up the limestone, At my entry to Spurn, over three hours later, the summer sun was high, flecking the Humber with dazzling white light.

My eyes followed the curving line of the peninsula to where a lighthouse rose with bands of black and white, like a stick of seaside rock. Barry Spence, Warden at Spurn for the Yorkshire Wildlife Trust, told me that from the entrance gate to the very tip of the peninsula the distance is about three and a-half miles.

Spurn is composed of sand, extending from cliffs of boulder clay. Barry said: "Sand is blown off the beach by the wind. It's trapped by the marram grass and dunes are formed. As they become thicker, a greater variety of plants takes root. Quite often, Spurn acts like an island. A rain shower heading towards it is affected by the convection currents and tends to go round. Spurn is one of the driest places in Britain."

On my last visit, in winter, when there was not enough wind to stir the marram grass, I watched two hundred brent geese, refugees from Siberia, feeding on zostera. Along the tideline was a generous sprinkling of wading birds – and anglers.

A concrete road, built by the Army, is the "spine" of the place, holding it together. The road, not the peninsula itself, is occasionally breached. The sea cut through it in March last year. The wind was not particularly strong, but a Force 12 storm in the sea further north created an enormous swell which, off the Yorkshire coast, combed with a high tide to batter the slender spit of land.

Spurn has been compared with a teardrop falling from the face of Yorkshire. It has a precarious existence. The main theory to account for the build-up and dispersal of the dunes which form this long peninsula is a cyclical process. It has been created and destroyed at intervals of about 200 years.

The formation of the next strip of sand is said to be along a line a little further west than its predecessor. Barry Spence lives near the root of the peninsula. He smiled as he said: "If anything happens, I'll be at the right side of any breach." Names for features at Spurn – Narrow Neck, Chalk Bank, Greedy Gut – hint at its precarious state.

Throughout the year, Spurn sees the comings and goings of day-trippers, naturalists, lifeboatmen, Humber pilots, anglers and the curious who, having scanned the map, notice that Spurn extends far into the Humber, as though intent on tickling the ribs of what we used to call Lincolnshire. It is fun to go to the furthest point.

The lifeboatmen and their families maintain a regular human presence near the tip of Spurn. The pilots come and go according to their duty roster. The coastguards departed to Bridlington in April, 1987.

Naturalists are thrilled by Spurn Point. I saw my first crossbills here. A highlight of 1988 was the re-appearance as a nesting species of the little tern. Three pairs nested. These were the first nests to be recorded for years, since a helicopter working for the Electricity Board made an unexpected landing in the small colony, on the point of Spurn.

On my August visit, I heard the creaky voices of migrant terns which were following shoals of small fish and being harrassed by three Arctic skuas. I saw a flock of knot in "breeding red", sanderlings from the Arctic, green and wood sandpipers from Scandinavia.

October brings wildfowl, notably the dark-breasted brent geese, about 200 birds, though up to 350 have been seen. The brent had left Spurn with the disappearance of the zostera, or eel grass, which is their staple food on the winter shore. These geese of the northlands came back to Spurn with the re-emergence of zostera rather more than ten years ago.

Scandinavian thrushes – redwings and fieldfares – arrive on this sandy shore in October and strip the orange berries from the buckthorn, a plant which provides good cover for the roe deer which have ventured here. In 1988, Barry saw a doe and two kids, the first proof of breeding in the locality.

The fox is well established throughout Spurn. Some foxes live under old buildings at the very point of the peninsula. Anglers seeking codling and whiting have told me of night-time fishing trips when they saw the eyes of foxes gleaming in torchlight.

One angler caught so many fish he simply threw them on to the beach for later collection. Foxes sneaked in and carried some of the fish away.

(1989)

MOORLAND DAYS

Bridestones: A Product of Wind, Frost and Rain

At least, the Bridestones are not associated with Wade, the ubiquitous giant of the North York Moors. It was Wade who dug out the Hole of Horcum, north of Pickering. He laid the causeway which most people now believe is a moorland stretch of a Roman road near Goathland.

If you must credit anyone with making the fungal-shaped Bridestones which straddle a ridge above Dovedale and Staindale, then perhaps it should be the Weather Clerk. Wind, frost and rain, over many centuries, have eaten away the moortop, leaving a few isolated fragments.

The Bridestones on a Heathered Ridge (Alec Wright)

The story goes that a newly-married couple found sanctuary in a recess near the base of one of the stones. It is an unlikely tale. What visitors to the Bridestones see are remnants of a much-eroded ridge. Some of the formations are like fungal growths when seen from a distance. All around are moors and conifer forest.

My expedition to the Bridestones began at Low Dalby, where the human population draws its income from the Forestry Commission. Here, a mile or two from Thornton Dale, is the start of the celebrated Forest Drive, a Backwoods experience which ends near Scarborough. A wind vane above the information centre showed in relief a horse-team drawing timber.

The abiding impression is of a gently undulating landscape, clad in conifers. A walker enters valleys which have names with a true northern ring about them – Sneverdale, Seivedale, Swairdale, Staindale. In the area are Stone Rigg and Dixon's Hollow, Cross Cliff and Bickley Gate.

The visitor is not only welcomed to Dalby Forest; he or she is cossetted. Here are picnic areas, car parks, toilets, telephones and standpipes for drinking water.

I met Bob and Jenny Dicker, wardens of the National Trust properties on the North York Moors. I was introduced to their two English springers, Hannah and Holly, plus six geese, eleven ducks, fifteen chicks and – a cat. Bob and Jenny took up their duties last spring, in dry and warm conditions. Since that time, the weather had been dismal, though not especially wet.

Said Jenny: "When we first arrived, it was minus 18 at night. We went for a walk with the dogs on one of those blue sky, crispy days. We walked to the Bridestones. Hannah, the old dog, likes to go into the beck and she was soaked. As she walked in the cold wind, we could hear ice jingling on her coat."

Bridestones Moor is run as a nature reserve. "Botanically, it is very interesting. We have acid, moorland type plants, also neutral type grass-land and some areas which are lime-rich. All in a small area. Some plants which occur up there are, to be honest, out of place. They thrive because lime has been washed down from exposures higher up."

We walked through Dovedale Griff, a "griff" being the local name for a small ravine carved by a moorland beck. We climbed through a knee-high growth of moorland plants. Patches of purple indicated where the bell heather was in bloom.

Competing for the peaty ground was bracken, which spreads insidiously by means of subterranean rhizomes and is hard to control when there are few cattle to trample it down nor spare human labour with scythes to shear it as bedding for young stock. Efforts have been made to spray the bracken.

The first of the Bridestones was that with a cave in which – it is said, tongue in cheek – a newly-married couple spent their first night: hence the name Bridestones.

Geologists will tell you the curious stones began to evolve through erosion. This affected the lower slopes, exposing cliffs composed of Jurassic sandstones which are alternately siliceous and cacareous, one band relatively strong and the other weak. A cliff was formed and, with further erosion, buttresses and eventually isolated outcrops came into being.

I was shown a grassed-over hummock which, in due course, would become an outcrop of naked rock. Given a few more thousand years of erosion and into being would come a Bridestone, which itself – in a time scale incomprehensible to the layman – would be gradually washed or blown away as particles of sand, to accumulate in the valley far below.

Weathering has disintegrated the calcareous rock faster than the siliceous. It gains entry into joints and along seepage lines, honeycombing the surface. A few plants – patches of heather and indomitable ferns – gain rootholds on the upstanding rock.

The "pedestal rock", which is portrayed on brochures and in books about the North York Moors, rose before us like a grotesque mushroom, some thirty feet high, with a wasp-waist of no more than fourteen feet. The Bridestones were continuing their slow deterioration, and the writer of an informative leaflet about this strange array of outcrops advised: "Enjoy them while you can!"

We left the dusty ridge and gained the moist stillness of native woodland, where bracken rose to a height of five feet and more. We slithered on the clay path and eventually reached the pleasantly cool kitchen of Low Staindale House, here to recuperate rapidly while sipping some freshly-brewed tea.

(1988)

Hutton-le-Hole: A Moorland Saunter

Autumn, on the North York Moors. Beyond the village and the farms; beyond the red pantiles and the rich brown masonry, the moorland wears its Joseph's coat of many colours. Apiarists have arrived with their stocks of bees to convert the nectar of the ling into honey which is so viscid it cannot be extracted from the combs by the usual means.

The breeding birds have drifted away; the grouse and the crows remain and will be joined in winter by parties of snow buntings, refugees from the northlands. Moorland sheep have been spained [the lambs separated from the ewes] and soon only the breeding stock will be on the moor, wearing out their teeth as they champ the tough heather plant.

Dr. Roy Brown, who heads the North York Moors National Park advisory services, tells me that as many as from ten to fifteen per cent of the sheep flock died early in the year under the wheels of speeding vehicles on unfenced moorland roads.

The remaining sheep were grazing between patches of bracken, a plant which has now encroached on 32,000 of the 125,000 acres of open ground. "It's a highly toxic plant and the bracken litter is the key environment for the nymph which is the penultimate stage in the development of the sheep tick," said Dr Brown, who leads a team of specialists and co-operates with kindred spirits, such as governmental bodies, industry, research institutes and landowners.

We walked towards Lastingham, along the edge of Spaunton Moor, written records for which go back to the time before the Conquest. These North York Moors are not especially high-lying, extending to no more than 1,400ft., yet the temperature may range from 35 to 40 degrees within 24 hours.

"On the high moors, we have recorded surface temperatures of plus 40 centigrade and a temperature as low as minus 20 centigrade. The moorland plants and animals must be highly adaptable."

I had thought of the North York Moors as having but a moderate rainfall and Roy admitted that most geography books support this view, some quoting an average annual fall of 40 inches. "Our researches show that in terms of the high moors, between 60 and 70 inches may be recorded, a figure made up of rainfall and some condensation. What can be said is that it is not as dry here as many people think."

Most of the moorland is privately owned. The owners are basically interested in grouse. The tenant farmers and others with ancient rights of common are concerned with the sheep. "So the presence of large numbers of flockmasters, as well as of sheep, is critical to the management of the moor."

We were greeted to the moor by an old ewe which, to judge by its markings, had come from Rosedale, almost eighteen miles away as the crow flies (if not as the sheep walks). "The area is an open sheep 'stray' and the sheep quickly discover that people may supply a supplementary source of food. Many sheep enter the car parks. This in itself can be innocent, but I have seen a horrendous case where a sheep, while inspecting a litter bin, put its nose on to a broken bottle."

Spaunton, a wet moor, is botanically rich, with a high population of insects to sustain a variety of moorland birds. "From a natural history point of view, this moor is one of the most important in the country." There is a good deal of diversity provided by the small valleys extending like fingermarks on to the moorland bloc.

The sheer extent of the moors is vital from the wildlife point of view. For instance, the North York Moors is one of the strongholds of the merlin in Britain, the area holding at least ten per cent of the breeding population. Along with the merlin exist the golden plover, curlew and many small ground-nesting birds.

It amused me to hear the crowing of a cock pheasant from the so-called grouse moor. "One of the trends over the last sixty years has been afforestation on the edge of the moors. I'm not talking just about big forests but various enterprises. An important part of the local economics is raising pheasants for shooting."

Roy added that the pheasant may not be the world's brightest bird, but it is not stupid and knows how to exploit the environment. "It is remarkable how many pheasants spend time on the moorland edge, often getting up to an elevation of over 1,000 ft."

One reason why the National Park became involved in moorland management was a spate of extensive fires in 1976. On Glaisdale Moor, a fire started in June burnt until September.

"The very deep peat has this peculiar history of wetting and drying. The fire got into an underground system of cracks . . . In some areas there was nothing apparently happening at the surface, but fire was quietly eating its way through some two or three feet down. We recorded surface temperatures of 900-1200 deg C."

We briefly left the road to explore part of Loskey Beck. In the calm between low-flying military jet aircraft, to which the wildlife of the Moors appears to have adjusted, we heard the metallic call of the local dipper . . .

(1988)

Farndale: Gold Amid the Purple

Farndale is a wait-and-see sort of place: deep-sunk, secluded. Local government split the dale into two, Farndale East and Farndale West, and the road pattern within the valley is a figure of eight, the crossing point being at Low Mills.

Socially, Farndale was always split into two: the upper and lower reaches. There is now a preponderance of old folk, one of whom told me: "It's all reight up here in summer, but as thou gets older it's a bigger struggle i' winter."

Here is a valley with the classic glacial U-shape. Walls and hedges form a framework which appears to have been designed to brace apart the moors. They are forever in the mind. It was from small quarries on those moors that the building material came – sandstone, roughly dressed, shaped into farm, cottage and also boundary walls made without mortar.

Farndale is one of a trio of north-south dales. Happily, only 1 in 10,000 of the day-trippers using the main road to Scarborough bother to turn off and seek out such remote little places.

Farndale is rather better known than the others because of a springtime profusion of daffodils, flowering among the alders by the River Dove – the "black or shady stream" of the Celtic folk. The daffodil colonies stretch for some seven miles along the banks of the Dove and its tributaries.

Daffodils were plucked by "hawkers", who took laden baskets to the nearby towns for sale. In 1955, the Ryedale branch of the Council for the Protection of Rural England made efforts to protect the plants. Now the blooms have legal protection. The County Council bye-law states that "no unauthorised person shall in the Farndale Nature Reserve uproot, cut or pluck or wilfully or negligently injure any daffodil or narcissus or the bud, stem or flower or leaf thereof".

Stone and Pantile in Farndale (Alec Wright)

The browns of native stone and reddish tones of roofing material give Farndale a warm appearance. The moors round about are empurpled with the flowering of ling in late summer. There is yellow in the colour scheme in spring when thousands of daffodils are in bloom.

The species is *Narcissus pseudonarcissus*. It is the small, wild daffodil of the type which grew by Ullswater, to be immortalised in William Wordsworth's famous poem. The Yorkshire daffodils have spread by seed propagation and the dispersal of bulbs by the river along its banks, where damp pastureland and the soils of Farndale provide ideal growing conditions.

A colourful explanation as to their origin – that the first bulbs were introduced by monks – lies in the realms of guesswork and folklore. The monastic association with Farndale is not in doubt, and the name of the valley first appeared as Fearnadale [an allusion to alders?] about 1154 in a charter granting the abbot and monks of Rievaulx Abbey a "clearing" in the dale. No one knowns when the daffodils appeared.

I mentioned at the beginning of this note the secluded nature of Farndale. The profusion and bonnie situation of daffodils give the valley an international renown. An old man related that at 8.45a.m. one April day he met two Dutch ladies at the car park near Low Mills. They had travelled overnight from the Continent specifically to see the daffodils.

Their verdict: "Much better than our tulip fields!"

(1988)

Gunnerside: A Sporting Estate

Red grouse talk to each other with deep, dry voices – *kowa, kowa*. Grouse are on subsistence rations through the long winter and into a tardy spring. Not until June do the high moors shrug off winter's chill and the grouse can take their pick from a variety of rich food.

Family coveys concentrate on the boggy places. Soon, the old cock birds are restive, ready to break away, to begin their territorial behaviour. Each August, the grouse are ritually culled, when a line of flag-waving men rouses the packs of birds and marksmen in butts lie in wait for the stubby-winged "moorcock".

To the Victorian gentry, who paid no income tax and had a reserve of cheap rural labour to sustain their large estates, grouse shooting was an enjoyable sport which did not need to make a profit. Lord Peel, at Gunnerside Lodge, high above the Swale, now has to reckon with modern business technology – with terms such as "cash flow". Grouse shooting is a strictly-controlled commercial proposition as well as a sport.

It was largely through Lord Peel's efforts that the Grouse Research Project came into being. A crucial aspect is burning tracts of rank old heather just before the nesting season to encourage the growth of new shoots, food for grouse and sheep. The Pennine moors are used as rough grazing for hill farming as well as for grouse shooting.

Lord Peel told me that east winds had come at the right time and dried out the moors. "In some years, burning may be restricted to three or four days." The son of a gamekeeper recalled being sent to the moor to "bray" the snow with a besom and expose the heath for the benefit of the grouse.

As Lord Peel spoke, he swivelled his office chair to point out features of the 32,000 acre estate on a map attached to the wall. The acreage sounds enormous, he said, but about 22,000 acres consist of commonland. As lord of the manor, he owns the freehold, but that is subject to the grazing rights of various farms: rights which are now stipulated under the Commons Registration Act.

The rest is in-bye land: either upland pasture or hay meadow. "I have the shooting over the 32,000 acres."

At the centre of the estate stands that "island hill" of Kisdon, behind which the Swale flows down a rock staircase. Lord Peel has a special fondness for Kisdon, a most characterful eminence. "From a grouse shooting point of view, it is also my favourite beat. It's a very small one. We don't let it commercially, but just keep it for ourselves – four or five guns only."

Lord Peel's father bought the estate from the son of Lord Rochdale in 1946. It had been Rochdale who, in the 1920s, developed a shooting lodge from a nucleus of old Dales buildings. "Being a shooting lodge,

which I took to be a polite way of saying it was dull. "You want a scree garden, not a rockery," he announced. And he promptly made me one.

I can see him now, labouring in the sunshine. He was stripped to the waist, his coarse khaki trousers held up by a pigskin belt and with his favourite beret on his head. I was looking at a man who retained his zest for life till the end.

Charles Graham spent some of his early years in the Army, having a spell with surveyors in the Himalayas. He was then not too far from an area frequented by Reginald Farrer. Mr Graham had almost forty years in industrial management, enjoying all of them – "frustrating committees, labour relations: the lot!" If the meeting was dull, he could always day-dream about his favourite hobbies: breeding tropical fish and rock-gardening. He knew most of the important gardeners of the North.

Retiring from work in 1964, he bought a plot of ground beside the Mains at Giggleswick and built a house, using up his surplus nervous energy in creating a garden, the full glory of which was unsuspected by those who simply walked up the Mains, for it was screened by a hedge, the drive climbed quite steeply and slipped behind more tall vegetation. To be invited to tour the garden was both an honour and a delight.

Making a garden gave him pleasure. Maintaining it was time-consuming. This deep-thinking man realised that "the end product for posterity will be just a few good trees." He looked around for other challenges and found one where Fell Beck has cut a deep bed for itself on its way from the heights of Ingleborough. In an area where an older rock peered through the limestone, Farrer planted many of the rhododendrons he found in the East.

Charles Graham knew that Farrer's rock garden in the village had been ruined and that yew trees had smothered the cliffside above Ingleborough Lake, the setting of an earlier attempt to rock-garden. Something might yet be done about the rhododendrons, though they had suffered from at least thirty years of neglect.

So Charles Graham went forth with saw and axe and fork – "a committee of one". He visited the gorge when he wanted; he did what he liked; he got peace of mind and job satisfaction; and he kept unsociable hours.

Joan Farrer recalls some elements of his daily routine. He was an "early bird" and the old blue car which only he was able to drive would arrive in the village as early as 6 a.m. The boot and floor of the car held a mass of assorted objects, from string to spade, and he would select what he required for his day's work.

He sauntered into the woods, carrying the implements and also a snack meal: cheese and dry bread. By 2-30 p.m., he was back in the village, setting off in his old blue car for his home, five miles away. Here he ate some boiled onions and slipped into bed for a couple of hours to rest and read. Mr Graham was an avid reader. "He had a thirsty mind," says Mrs Farrer.

On his first jaunts to the rhododendron groves, he felled any unwanted sycamores, hazels and birches, developing the technique of using a rope to swing along the sides of the gorge with saw and axe, clinging to the part he wished to clean up. He would then descend to beck level to remove a tangle of fallen logs.

He found seedlings which had lodged in moss or between tree roots. Some, which were struggling in crannies in the outcropping slate, were transported from Clapham to Giggleswick, here to be given nursery conditions until he judged it wise to return them to the wild. He would show me his little nursery plot beside the house, reciting like a litany the scientific names for the plants.

The seedlings grown in pans were transferred to peat beds. By 1983, some of his re-introduced rhododendrons were four feet high and in flower. On winter evenings, he classified species of rhododendron from his collection of transparencies. A typical entry in his record is: *Rhododendron wardii 1970 . . . East bank. High above the pump house. Not seen since.*

The letters he wrote to Joan Farrer about the plants are models of style and coherence. She had mentioned Dianthus. He replied:

> *Dear Mrs Farrer,*
> *James Douglas was one of the foremost raisers of Dianthus, the other was Montague Allwood of Allwood Bros., Haywards Heath, Sussex. I have bought from both but prefer Douglas for Hardy Dianthus, excluding alpines.*
>
> *Avoid Mrs Sinkins and its improvements because although it has, perhaps, the strongest scent of any pink, the flower is full, the calyx splits and the habit is therefore untidy.*

Another time he wrote:

> *For your consideration – Bluebells. On the left bank about opposite the waste bin leading down to the pump house, if bluebells could be established there they would catch the eye before the Rhododendrons.*

One afternoon, Charles Graham arrived at the back door of Hall Garth, home of the Farrers, in some distress. A tree had rolled on him. He had walked back to the village using the shaft of his fork as a crutch. After that incident, he was laid up at home for six weeks, but kept mentally busy, spending part of the time naming the plant-paintings which Farrer made on his journeys.

Charles Graham died in 1986 at the age of 87. The Clapham project was a worthy culmination of his long and richly varied life.

(1987)

Blacktoft Sands:
Birds Among the Rustling Reeds

T he village of Blacktoft lies east of Goole and to the north of the River Ouse. It seemed reasonable to drive here to visit Blacktoft Sands. "If thou does that, thou'll be wastin' time," said a genial resident of Goole. "T'Sands is on t'other side." I crossed the river bridge.

I was visiting the top corner of a former great fen. Three or four centuries ago, it stretched unbroken from south-east Yorkshire down through Cambridgeshire into East Anglia. Drained by the industrious Dutch, it is now a tract of top-quality arable land. The rustle of the reeds has given way to the rustle of wheat stalks.

Andrew Grieve, warden at the bird reserve of Blacktofts, mentioned the former marshy state of the land. The people lived in hamlets connected by causeways which were usable in summer. In winter, the area was extensively flooded. The residents used reeds to thatch their houses and augmented their food supplies by slaughtering the numerous waterfowl.

The Fens were undoubtedly an ornithologist's paradise. The boom of

Reeds and Salt Water by the Humber

Many species of bird settle to rest and re-fuel at the reed-beds and lagoons of Blacktoft Sands, where the horizon is low, the land claimed by agriculture is almost as smooth as a billiards table and the day is regulated by the ebb and flow of the tidal water. Blacktoft is managed as a nature reserve and "hides" are provided for visitors, who can thus watch the birds without being seen.

the bittern would be heard and marsh harriers were doubtless common. Old records mention species such as the spoonbill, purple heron and black tern. In winter, the sky was clouded by thousands of immigrant duck. Nowadays, an arable landscape looks so flat it might have been created using a spirit level.

Having crossed the bridge from Goole, I found myself in an area of neat villages, with a grassed-over embankment containing the tidal Ouse. Navigational aids for shipping were incongruous in the farmland setting.

Swinefleet and Reedness, Whitgift and Ousefleet – these were enchanting names for the villages through which I drove. Norsefolk named some of the settlements. They had turned the prows of their longboats into the Humber and had used the Ouse for swift passage to the heart of Yorkshire.

Blacktoft Sands bird reserve of the RSPB lies at the confluence of the two rivers. From that point onwards it becomes the Humber estuary. "The River Trent comes in from the south and the River Ouse from the west. It is an area of foreshore; a big tide flowing up the Humber floods the whole reserve."

A wall built alongside a low-lying mudbank in the 1920s was an attempt to keep the river free of silt for navigation. Silt was deposited on the mud. The level of the mudbank rose quickly and by 1945 vegetation had spread right across it. So there developed a big new reed-bed, "a throw-back, if you like, to the old fenland habitat which had once existed."

The reserve extends over 460 acres. Conditions are salty and thus three-quarters of the area is covered by reed. A few lagoons and ponds were excavated and a few trees planted. "There is a bit more variety now, but basically it is flat and open, one of the largest continuous reed-beds in the country."

The warden and I stood on the floodbank overlooking what appeared to be a continuous mass of reeds. A red-painted lighthouse in the distance marked where the Trent and Ouse were blending their waters. Houses on the skyline were in the village of Blacktoft.

The first "hide" we visited overlooked a lagoon which had been lowered to provide shallow water and wet mud for the visiting waders – dunlin, probably from Scandinavia, ringed plover, a curlew sandpiper from Eastern Russia, doubtless heading for wintering grounds in West Africa.

A few ruff were visible. More dunlin arrived, their underwings gleaming white in the bright light as they banked, to alight beside one of several artificial islands made to encourage nesting birds. In summer, such islands attract Canada geese, mute swans, mallard and gadwall.

A well-filled lagoon held several hundred mallard and some teal. Wading birds included a black-tailed godwit. Bearded tit and reed warbler nest in the area. Bitterns from the Continent are seen in winter.

Temminck's stint and wood sandpiper are among the rarities which touch down at Blacktoft Sands on their way north to breed. "It's a quick turnabout with waders," said Andrew. "Then they all start coming back." Some black terns show themselves on their way to Continental nesting grounds.

Blacktoft Sands, thirty-eight miles from the open sea, has attracted bird species usually associated with the coast. Among the sightings was a puffin, being chased over farmland by a sparrow hawk. No one could tell me the end of this fascinating story.

(1989)

Wheldrake:
Water Meadows of the Derwent

"**W**e have some superb meadows," said Tim Dixon. "In June, there seem to be more flowers than grass." He was referring to the Ings of the lower Derwent Valley and to Wheldrake Ings in particular. These four hundred acres have scarcely changed their appearance in the span of a thousand years.

The name Ings is part of the Norse bequest and it means "water meadows" – riverside land which floods in the winter and from which in summer a crop of grass is taken as hay. Tim, who is a scientist and nature reserve warden employed by the Nature Conservancy Council, reminded me that since the 1939-45 war, the country has lost ninety-seven per cent of its lowland hay meadows.

Wheldrake Ings, south-east of York, has been a meadow since before the compilation of Domesday Book. It endures in a natural state. "Water meadows" may be seen on both sides of the river between Newton and Breighton.

Ian Kibble, who presides over the management committee of Wheldrake Ings, most of which is owned by the Yorkshire Wildlife Trust, described for me this flat area of alluvial clay which extends to the former course of the Derwent. It is crossed by dykes which allow some control of winter flooding.

"The grassland communities of the reserve are almost unique through an absence of any agricultural chemicals and through the traditional form of management – hay-cropping and grazing. The land is enriched by the river silt which comes with the winter floods." The Ings have never been ploughed.

John Jackson, of Poplar Tree Farm, handed me a tuft of hay he had tugged from a bale in his Dutch barn. This hay came from the Ings. A few bales remained from the 1986 crop. I teased some strands, then sniffed at it, inhaling the aroma of last summer. A greenish tinge signified that the hay had been taken in good weather.

Tim Dixon called the Ings "an anachronistic landscape which has

retained many of the plants and animals which were formerly widespread."
This Yorkshire prairie is not uniformly green, like a modern meadow, but
smudgy with pastel shades and including "marshy bits" where the sieves
[rushes] grow. Specialists look for such plant celebrities as sneezewort,
pepper saxifrage and dropwort.

I watched John Jackson locate a boundary stone. He carried a fork
and used the end of the shaft to thump the ground. A "clunk" was
heard as the shaft came down on a stone, now covered with a mat of
verdant sward. It was a quite ordinary stone and I had expected something special – something standing proud, carrying the initials of one of
the old Wheldrake families.

"Nearly everybody had a bit of land and paid their dues to Escrick. The
pub had an acre, the butcher had an acre. Any which were not taken up
one year were 'sold' at the brig... I'm lucky. I have some of the best
ground. There's all sorts in it, but it makes good hay. When you get
further out, it can be very seggy [infected with rushes]."

At Wheldrake Ings, the hay is usually taken off by the second week in
July. Then the cattle and sheep are driven on to the aftermath to graze
until the end of October, by which time the ground is becoming soggy.
If the stock was left much longer, the hoovers would cut up the land.

The Ings normally flood in November, and it is then that the great
hordes of wildfowl arrive, finding sanctuary and food during the winter.

Tim Dixon recalled an autumn morning when, at his home in North
Duffield, he could hear water pouring over the banks of the Derwent
about a mile away. "When there's a really big flood – when its topping
the banks – it makes a strange rushing noise which carries a long way.
Get up to it and it's terrifying – a great wall of water gushing down into
the Ings. It is dangerous to go near it."

Tim feels a shiver of excitement when, afar off, he hears the wild musical
trumpeting calls of the first Bewick's swans to return to Derwent Valley
after nesting in Siberia. In their winter quarters, the swans tend to stay in
a large flock. "To see two hundred birds coming in to roost on a winter
afternoon – just planing down to alight on the water – is memorable."

The annual flooding of the valley is spectacular. For several months,
one has been aware of an overall greenness. Almost overnight, the waters
spread and now there is the gunmetal-grey of the extensive floods.

The first ducks to arrive (in August and early September) are teal.
Wigeon appear in October and November, which is about the same time
as the Bewick's swans. In a normal winter, between 120 and 200 of these
far northern swans are present.

The largest number recorded by Tim Dixon was 270. "They will stay
right through a freeze-up. If the Ings are solid ice, the birds go on to the
river to feed. This is an area of international importance, protected under
EEC legislation. We had had in February up to 20,000 wildfowl."

Birdwatchers who clump across the Bailey Bridge follow a path beside the Derwent and, from a hide beside the river, have a wide view of the Ings and the massed birds. Wigeon swirl in the air. The floodwater holds large parties of mallard and teal, dining on the rhizomes of marsh plants, particularly reed grass and iris. They also take the seeds of plants. On the sodden fringes are waders, among them lapwing and golden plover.

Roland Patrick, a local farmer, told me: "When a flood is expected, we put a stick in the ground as a marker. Sometimes the water is level with yon gate top . . . It's reckoned that when the valley floods reight, there's a twenty-five mile stretch o' watter."

The Ings are "a terrible" place in gusty weather. The wind meets no resistance on the Derwent flatlands, near the geographical heart of Old Yorkshire.

(1987)

BEATING THE BOUNDS

These articles were published prior to 1974, when the Boundary Commission played fast and loose with the county border, giving chunks of historic Yorkshire to our neighbours. Those born in Old Yorkshire regard such lost territory as being out on loan.

Mickle Fell: Crowning the Northern Skyline

Yorkshire extends a finger of land to tickle the ribs of Westmorland. The list of Yorkshire highspots is headed by Mickle Fell, a grassy ridge where an untidy cairn stands at a height of 2,591 ft. Mickle Fell is thus not much bigger than Whernside (2,414ft), which occupies second place in the list.

Mickle Fell presides over England's last great wilderness, to the north of the road between Brough and Middleton-in-Teesdale. There is no really easy way to Mickle Fell – unless, and heaven forbid, you have access to a helicopter. The approaches from Grains o' Beck, from the Tees or from Westmorland, involve a slog during which your boots will fill with peat-brown water and your leg muscles become as taut as violin strings.

If I felt any trepidation at the thought of covering those High Pennine miles, it was not because of the physical effort but on seeing a notice within a few yards of where I left the scar in Hilton, one of several little "ton" villages on the East Fellside. I had decided to climb Mickle Fell from the Westmorland side and was about to enter an Army training area.

About 40,000 acres were taken over by the military during the 1939-45 war and several million pounds were spent on concrete roads, tank parks and gun emplacements. The area includes the lost hamlet of Burton, birthplace of Christopher Bainbridge, who in 1508 became Archbishop of York.

The Army range is tenanted by footloose sheep, ravens and buzzards. My old friend Bill Robson, on being granted permission to explore the area, found a pair of wheatears nesting down the gun barrel of a redundant tank.

I had written authority to enter the range. No red flag was flying. I heard no distant boom of a gun, no high-pitched whine of a shell in transit. I sniffed the air for the tang of cordite, but there was only the rich flavour of peat, wafted down by the gentlest of breezes.

The track I followed had an easy gradient, keeping close to the beck in a larger-than-usual Pennine gill which had possibly been hewn out by overspill from a glacial lake around what is now Maize Beck. It was tempting to stop and pick up samples of minerals from spoil heaps associated with lead-mining.

I climbed close to the stream and reached the narrow watershed between Hilton and Swarth Becks. Then came the most tiring stretch – peat and rushes, heather and sphagnum, across a landscape where the horizons were low and afar off. The peat had been wind-eroded into thick pats. Here and there, tufts of heather appeared to erupt as grouse took flight, leaving moulted feathers behind them.

Mickle Fell crowned the horizon to the east. It was a big, smooth lump, with none of the savage grandeur one might expect from the highest point in England's largest county. A Stirling bomber came down during the last war and for some years before it was removed, one of the light alloy girders within the fuselage was used as a nesting place by a pair of ring ouzels, our white-bibbed "mountain blackbirds".

From the sprawling summit cairn I looked into Birkdale, with its lonely farm, set close to the Pennine Way. Light glinted on Maize Beck, which joins the river Tees close to Cauldron Snout and Falcon Clints.

The residents of Birkdale found themselves in a Westmorland parish. To visit Dufton, they followed the old track through the Pennines via High Cup Nick. When Grannie died at Birkdale, her body was strapped to the back of a fell pony. On reaching Dufton, with time in hand, the pony was tethered and the family mourners went into the inn for a drink.

They emerged to find the pony had slipped its halter and was on its way back to Birkdale Farm where, if the story is to be believed, the children who had been left in the care of a adult saw the returning pony with its precious burden and said, delightedly: "Grannie's coming back!"

(1967)

Croft: Lewis Carroll's Yorkshire Wonderland

The Tees is the boundary between the North Riding and County Durham. In 1843, the Rev. Charles Dodgson arrived at Croft, on the Yorkshire bank, with a large but young family. Croft was a desirable Crown living, having been made available by the Prime Minister, Sir Robert Peel.

When Parson Dodgson died a quarter of a century later, he might simply

have been another name on the long list of Croft Rectors. He acquired
fame not through his own efforts but because one of his numerous offspring
was a brilliant mathematician, an Oxford don and the writer of one of
the world's most enduring books for children. He was christened Charles
Lutwidge Dodgson but is best-known as Lewis Carroll, author of *Alice
in Wonderland*.

It astonished me that at Croft enough remains of the place for anyone
interested in Lewis Carroll's youth to be able to evoke the place as it was
a century and a quarter ago. Here, only a few miles from the heart of
Darlington and from the incessantly busy Great North Road, time has not
stood still, but it does not seem to have been in any special hurry. The old
road from Northallerton to Darlington still crosses the water on a bridge
of pointed and ribbed arches.

Long before the Dodgsons settled at the 34-room, red-brick Rectory,
Croft was noted for the mineral content of its water. In 1713, Londoners
were reported to be paying large sums for sealed bottles of the liquid.
Parson Dodgson saw a newly-built hotel crowded with visitors to the Spa.
His Rectory must have seemed like a hotel, forever busy, for he had ten
children, with a stipend of £900 a year for their maintenance. Since his
time, a whole wing has been demolished without loss of appeal.

From the window of the Rector's study, I looked across the lawn to the
acacia tree under which Lewis Carroll lay on sunny days – he called it his
"umbrella tree" – and where he wrote a good deal of his early work.
He edited a family magazine called *The Rectory Umbrella*. In the present
Rector's study I saw a photograph of the large Dodgson family, its members
dispersed across the lawn.

Croft church was already ancient when Lewis Carroll knew it. There
is no memorial to him. The Rector's brainy son must have seen the
Milbankes drive to church in state from Hanlaby Hall. He was familiar
with the vast family tomb, made of marble and lying in the shadow of
their magnificent pew.

The mind boggles at the sight of the Milbanke pew. In an age when
everyone had a place in society, and kept to that place, members of the
Milbanke family mounted a wide staircase, between twisted balusters, to
gain entry to a pew which was held aloft on fluted columns. It was almost
a home from home, being decked out with red beige and curtains.

Since the Dodgson days, the south aisle has lost its gallery. The pews
known to Lewis Carroll have twice been replaced, first with pitch pine and
then with oak. Stained glass has replaced plain glass in the west window.

The young man who was to become world famous as the author of *Alice
in Wonderland* was a pupil at Richmond Grammar School, some ten miles
from Croft, where his flair for mathematics was quickly detected by the
Headmaster, who told the lad's father "you may fairly anticipate for him
a bright career."

Young Dodgson moved on to Rugby, thence to Oxford. Although there is a trickle of admirers to the village on the banks of the Tees, most literary buffs head for Christ Church, Oxford, and the river on which, during a summer outing, the young don told his fantastic tales about Alice – tales which he was persuaded to jot down. Later in life, when mad about photography, he turned up at the Rectory with cumbersome camera and bulky equipment.

The old parson died in 1868. He and his wife share a grave in Croft churchyard. It is surrounded by wrought iron railings. The famous son failed to reach Croft in time to say a last farewell to either parent. When father had died, the rest of the family left Croft for "The Chestnuts" in the Guildford area.

A direct link with the family ended not long ago. A villager who died in 1962 had recalled when Skeffington Dodgson, the youngest son of the Rector, had passed her in the street and suddenly burst into a trot, running for about two hundred yards. Asked later about his unexpected sprint, Skeffington said: "I always run that little bit."

Lewis Carroll (courtesy of National Portrait Gallery)

Lewis Carroll was the pseudonym of the son of a clergyman who for many years served the parish of Croft, by the Tees. Carroll, a brilliant mathematician, became world famous for his imaginative account of Alice's adventures down a rabbit hole.

Lewis Carroll was more familiar with the intellectual circles of Oxford than with the quiet village by the Tees, but Croft has not forgotten him. Its history has been a long one, but no personality from it shines more brightly than the man who directed Alice down a rabbit hole – and thought of curious and highly entertaining adventures for her in Wonderland.

(1965)

Slaidburn: a Yorkshire Shangri-la

The name "Forest of Bowland" hints at woodland on a grand medieval scale. The old Bowland Rural District Council added to the romanticism by devising road signs adorned by the silhouette of a chubby little archer in the act of drawing on his bow.

First-footers in Bowland half expect to see a sort of annexe to Sherwood Forest, with homes grouped in clearings and the men wearing tunics of green. The air holds the whiff of woodsmoke and the subtler aroma of cooked venison.

So much for the romance. The Forest of Bowland, a Norman concept, was land set aside for hunting by the king and his favourites. It might or might not be well-wooded. In due course, the deer were emparked and agricultural interests got the upper hand. The old name was Bolland, said to mean "land of cattle". In medieval times, cattle were ranched at vaccaries, or clearings. Towards the end of the forest period, land-hungry farmers pressed hard at the perimeter.

Slaidburn, the highest of three settlements in the Hodder Valley, was one of the places where forest law was upheld. The old courtroom furniture survives at a local inn. Slaidburn, for many years an estate village, has not altered much for years. Viewed from the road across the Hodder, it looks grey and mysterious – a Yorkshire Shangri-la.

This village grew up beside a trackway leading to a crossing of the Hodder, which here receives an infusion of cold water from Croasdale Beck. Slaidburn is a drawn-out, relatively thin village, resembling a letter T with a long stem.

Here you can be stimulated rather than oppressed by a weight of history. I visited a large house, where the welcome included a cup of coffee, and heard that when the building was re-occupied in 1948 it had been empty though fully-furnished for seventy years. Some curtains, and even carpets, in use today are a hundred years old.

A snack at the *Hark to Bounty* was doubly enjoyable because of the setting. I reclined on an eighteenth century oak settle. Fire glowed in a dog grate and brought a responsible sparkle from a copper kettle. The old courtroom, with its venerable furnishings, served a copyhold or manor court and was functioning up to 1920. (Mrs King-Wilkinson has a painting which – she believes – is of Bounty, the hound belonging to old Mr Wrigglesworth, of Town Head). Bounty's melodious calls provided the name for the sole remaining inn.

Visiting St. Andrew's Church, in what is claimed to be England's largest parish (sixty-five square miles), I was told that the three-decker pulpit is still used in its original way, with the clerk occupying the bottom deck, the Rector taking the service from the second deck and, clad in black gown with "tabs", preaching from the top deck.

Slaidburn is so far behind the times in some respects that the wheel of fashion has come a full circle. There is no altar as such. A communion table is "free standing", in the spirit of the Reformation.

At Slaidburn, tales are told of the men who dammed the upper Hodder valley to form Stocks reservoir for the benefit of the thirsty Fylde of Lancashire. The 1920s were stormy as navvies drank or fought. Some of them curled up for sleep in the gigantic pipes which were to be laid underground. A kindly family organised a soup kitchen for them at the village hall.

Slaidburn has a closely-knit community. Mrs King-Wilkinson told me of her youngest daughter's wedding in 1965. Everyone in the village took part in some way. The cake was made by a farmer's daughter. Another young woman helped with the clothes. Five hundred people attended the wedding and those who were not guests turned up to assist with the reception.

Slaidburn's general insularity was produced by centuries of isolation. In some respects, it is insular still and there is a quite remarkable pride in the locality. It has an ageing population ("half the folk could die off tomorrow," I was told).

There was a quiet resolution on the part of everyone I met that no radical changes must take place.

(1968)

Todmorden: White and Red Roses

Think of Todmorden as a letter Y. The stem of the letter is a main cut through the Pennines. The forks are valleys, one leading to Rochdale and the other to Burnley. There's hardly any valley land, which means that the buildings of Tod jostled for whatever land was spare when road, canal and railway had claimed the best strips.

Two Pennine terms used locally are *uplands* for the grassy parts – those high pastures ribbed with walls and dotted with farms that look half as old as time – and *moors* for the heathery bits, where peat is thick and black.

I arrived at the Todmorden Municipal Offices at coffee time, but there was no coffee for me. I was told it was being served in the Mayor's Parlour

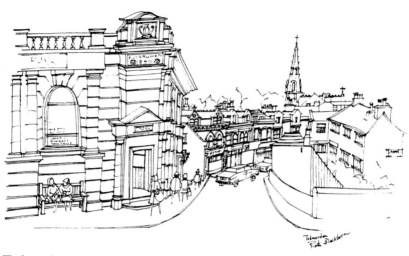

Todmorden (Ruth Blackburn)

Stone riven from the local hills gives Todmorden a permanent feel. The industrialised town has a principal hall built in a Grecian style. Beneath the hall flows the river Calder, the former county boundary.

at the Town Hall, just across the street. This was one of several unexpected but pleasant memories of a visit to Yorkshire's best-known frontier town.

Todmorden is not much to look at – unless you have a passion for early Victoriana, industrial division. Bill Holt, a globe-trotting author who was born at Todmorden and returned to live in the area, said: "Tod's not an oil painting, by any means, but the surrounding moors are beautiful." When visiting Germany, he discovered that Todmorden, as two words, means "dead murder".

William Holt was born in a terraced house in Joshua Street and, by wielding the pen, has bought an Elizabethan manor house. He said he returned to live at Todmorden because he likes Todmorden folk. "They are very sincere, warm-hearted, genuine." He was accompanied by Trigger, the white horse he bought after it had experienced a life of drudgery pulling a rag and bone cart.

Across the main valley from Stoodley, where a monument stands up with the visual impact of an exclamation mark, is the hill called Whirlaw, which Bill Holt used as the setting for a recent book, *The Wizard of Whirlaw*.

Todmorden has a worsted factory, established here by one of the best-known firms of the West Riding. Wool figured early in the industrial story of the place through the activities of Joshua Fielden, farmer-cum-tycoon, who went into cotton spinning.

The fact that he had five zestful sons was to give the family local renown. Fielden money not only brought mills into being but created public buildings. The Town Hall, opened in 1891, was a Fielden embellishment. Built ponderously, in a classical style, it might have strayed here from Greece but for its millimetre of ingrained soot.

The town had its Fielden School of Art and a Unitarian Church in the Decorated style of Gothic. The latter building cost the Fieldens £53,000. It dominates not only Fielden Square but half the town as well.

Pioneering is a Todmorden characteristic. Openshaws were among the world's first manufacturers of knitted fashion piece goods in such fabrics as Courtelle, Acrilan and Crimplene. The main business today is with speciality cloths for the lithographic printing industry.

Socially, the Todmordians have a genius for entertaining themselves. The list of amateur organisations is almost at arm's length. There is even a small theatre in town, a building which started off life as a theatre, then became a cinema and, on its closure, was rented by the Todmorden Players. The recently-renovated Town Hall is vast and is sometimes used by the BBC Northern Orchestra for concerts which are broadcast live or are recorded for future programmes.

If a riot breaks out at Todmorden, it is most likely to be over cricket than some social evil. Johnny Wardle has said that the cricket ground at Todmorden is one of the loveliest in the world.

There is no brooding on the past. Billy Holt, the author, told me the town is so ungrateful that no one knew where one of its principal bene-factors, John Fielden, was buried until he [Mr Holt] found the grave, covered with weeds, near the Unitarian Sunday School.

After world-wide travels, Billy Holt – and the faithful Trigger – returned to their roots, to the Yorkshire town which has red and white roses on its coat of arms. (Let is be whispered that the red rose is uppermost.)

The borough of Todmorden is now wholly in the West Riding of Yorkshire. The Mayor reminded me that in the old days a dancer at Todmorden Town Hall, which was built above the river Calder, the county boundary, might have one foot in Yorkshire and one in Lancashire.

Todmorden has a setting of space and grandeur. I had a feeling that anyone who lives here feels like a freeman without going through the formality of receiving a scroll at an official ceremony.

Its border state has given Todmorden an excess of enthusiasm for Yorkshire. "Aye, lad," said one of its sons, "when thou's so near t'enemy, thou's inclined to give thi tail a reight good wag."

(1967)

A Postscript

After fifty years of travel and inquiry, I feel I am beginning to know the county of York.

Yorkshire is vast and varied. Its beauty is more than skin deep, as the explorers of caves and potholes in the north-west will testify. The main chamber of Gaping Gill, Ingleborough, has a scale to rival York Minster – plus a lively beck, which pours over a lip of limestone to descend for 340 ft to a pebbly floor.

Motoring from my home at Giggleswick to the cliffs overlooking the North Sea – and travelling against the grain of the landscape – I have marvelled at the contrasting scenes. There has been the thrill of personal discovery – the remains of old abbeys and the half-forgotten villages tucked away in folds between the hills.

It has been a joy to explore Old York, to shop in market towns like Ripon or Northallerton and, in the milltowns of the west, to become aware of Yorkshire's role in the industrial revolution, which filled many a valley with the sooted magnificence of large textile mills.

Folk are more important than things. I recall with special pleasure my encounters with Yorkshire folk, who are so varied in their speech, manners and occupations, and yet are united by a love for their native county.

There's none better.